The Amateur Taxidermist

The Amateur Taxidermist

A Step-by-Step Illustrated Handbook on
How to Stuff and Preserve
Birds, Fish, and Furred Animals

Jean Labrie

HART PUBLISHING COMPANY, INC.
NEW YORK CITY

TRANSLATED FROM THE FRENCH BY FLORENCE WALL

Copyright © 1972 by Hart Publishing Company, Inc.

All rights reserved

No part of this book may be reproduced in any form
without written permission from the publisher.

SBN Number 8055-1035-4

Library of Congress catalog card number 75-186668

Printed in the United States of America

Contents

The Amateur Taxidermist

Introduction

TAXIDERMY is the art of preparing and preserving the skins of dead animals. The taxidermist attempts to make the preserved animal resemble the living creature as closely as possible. To do this, he undertakes four successive operations: (1) skinning the animal, (2) treating the skin with a chemical protective preparation, (3) stuffing the skin, and (4) mounting the completed specimen. These four stages will be treated in detail in this book.

The amateur taxidermist, like the professional, must be patient and persevering. He should practice often and thoroughly, with as little interruption as possible. In this way, he will enjoy the rewards of this absorbing and remunerative skill.

Obtaining a Specimen

BEFORE you go out to look for a specimen prepare yourself well on the subject. A dictionary or an encyclopedia will be very useful. Books on animals are excellent sources of information. The municipal libraries are also sources highly valued by naturalists and by the friends of animals. Set up an index of photographs and personal notes that you can consult easily.

Specimens can be obtained from several sources. Among your friends there may be several hunters and fishermen who will offer you some of their catch.

Hunting

If you have the opportunity to go into the woods you will surely find what you need. Note that crows are excellent subjects for taxidermy.

Do not kill birds that are protected by the government. You will find a list of these in information on the hunting of migrant birds.

Rifles, Carbines, Ammunition

The less the animal is damaged, the easier it will be to stuff it. You must therefore use the appropriate ammunition for each case. Thus to shoot a squirrel do not use a 12-caliber rifle, loaded with buckshot. Instead, use No. 7½ bullets, or a 22-caliber carbine.

My preferred rifle is a 410-caliber, with which I use 3-inch cartridges with No. 7½ or No. 6 shot. Do not forget that the bigger the number, the smaller the shot.

For big game, I use a 30-30 Winchester, model 94. I also recommend a 308 or a 30-06.

Precautions and Preparations

If you shoot the animal yourself, try to damage it as little as possible. The stuffing will then be much easier.

Be sure to follow these five basic rules:

1. Observe the position of the animal before shooting it; this will be useful when you stuff it.

2. *Never aim at the head.* You could shatter the skull, and you would then have to reconstruct it later.

3. As soon as the animal is killed note the color of the eyes. (Always have a notebook with you when you go to the woods or to a zoo.)

4. As soon as possible, pack with wadding the openings through which blood or excrement could escape.

5. Wipe the fur or plumage carefully with wadding, so that the blood will not coagulate on it. It is very difficult to remove it later.

If after shooting a small bird you find it has been only wounded, finish it by placing your hand under the wing and compressing the thorax with your fingers for a few seconds. This has the effect of stopping the circulation of the blood and the respiration. For bigger birds, a second shot will not damage the specimen.

Never skin a bird right after it has been killed. The reason for this is simple: if, by an unlucky cut of scalpel or knife, you press too hard in making the abdominal incision, the blood, which has not yet coagulated, will run out and flood the plumage. It is therefore preferable to wait until the bird is completely cold.

After obtaining a specimen, if you do not have the time to work on it immediately, put it in the freezer—*never in the refrigerator.* Leave it there until the evening before the day you will work on it so that it can thaw during the night. Take note, naturally, of the size of the animal, because it is obvious that the bigger it is, the more time it will take to thaw.

Tools and Materials

In your work as an amateur taxidermist you will need a place where you can easily stuff the animals that you have collected. It is advisable to have a window above your worktable. Half a vacant garage, a well-lighted basement, space in an attic, would serve the purpose, although the ideal place would be a studio especially constructed for taxidermy. My place always has some chairs for interested spectators, and they are rarely unoccupied.

TOOLS

Many types of tools and instruments are available for both the amateur and the professional taxidermist. You should use your ingenuity in obtaining the necessary equipment.

Start with the following:

1 small metal brush	1 penknife
1 pair of scissors	1 tweezer
1 hammer	1 nipper
1 tack hammer	1 vise
1 cross-cut saw	1 brush with soft hairs
1 aluminum comb	1 hooker and some hooks
1 saw for making strips	1 spool of nylon cord
1 pair of shears	Modeling clay

Artificial eyes

Brushes and some oil paint of best quality in a tube

1 bottle (3 oz.) hydrocholoric acid

1 assortment of galvanized wires

1 assortment of sewing needles and nonputrefying thread

1 scalpel: No. 3 handle, No. 10 blade

Boiled linseed oil (bought in hardware stores)

Nails, tacks, scraps of wood

Cotton for stuffing; padding

Some straw (kind used by glazers and packers)

Plaster of Paris, paste, table salt

With these supplies, I succeeded very well with my first specimens. As you acquire more experience, you will discover other useful tools.

Fig. 1. Staple gun tacker No. T-55 (Arrow).

Fig. 2. Long spatula (used for remodeling skulls with papier-mache).

Fig. 2A. Assorted artificial eyes (large eyes are deer eyes).

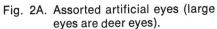

Fig. 2B. Spool of waxed thread (the kind used by shoemakers).

Fig. 2C. Straight scissors
(5½ inches long).

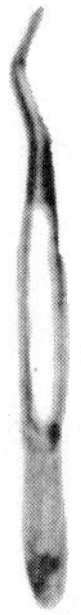

Fig. 2F. Flat-nosed
forceps with
broad tip (4
inches
long).

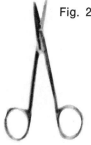

Fig. 2D. Straight
scissors (4
inches long).

Fig. 2G. Scalpel
handle No. 3.

Fig. 2H. Scalpel blade
No. 10.

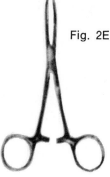

Fig. 2E. Skin holder
(with locked
handle).

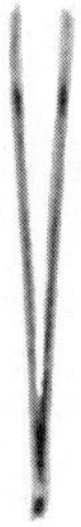

Fig. 2J. Needle-pointed
straight forceps.

Fig. 2K. Straight forceps (5 inches long).

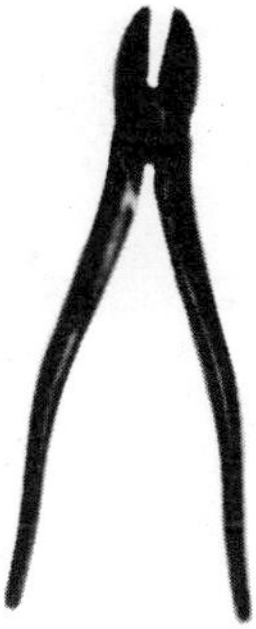

Fig. 2N. Side cutters (for wires).

Fig. 2L. Two knitting rods of different size.

Fig. 2P. Hunting knife blade (5 inches long).

Fig. 2M. Screwdriver.

Fig. 2Q. Surgeon's needles.

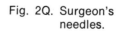

Fig. 2R. Bone saw (24 inches long).

Fig. 2S. Rubberized
        tape measure
        (60 inches long).

Fig. 2T. Paint scraper (10
        inches long).

Fig. 2U. Bone snip (8 inches long).

Fig. 2V. Spool of thread (for sewing).

Fig. 2X. Skin adjuster (8 inches long).

Fig. 2Y. Pocket knife (4½ inches long).

Materials

You will also need various materials for preparing the specimen. Here are some basic materials with instructions for producing them.

Papier-Máché

Liquid paste	3 oz.
Newspaper	10 oz.
Plaster of Paris	20 oz.

Tear the newspaper into little pieces, and put them into a bucket full of warm water. Let the mixture soak for 48 hours; then press the paper to extract the water.

Prepare the paste from flour, using 1 part of flour to 2 parts of water. Boil it until it is the consistency of starch.

Mix paste and paper and add the Plaster of Paris. Knead the mass as you would knead dough for bread. To color it, add some paint, in powder form or from a tube.

Asbestos Powder

This powder can be bought wherever materials for construction are sold.

Put a few handfuls into a vessel and add enough water to produce a workable mixture. Shape this material into the form that you have chosen, and let it harden for several days. A source of heat (radiator, hot air) will accelerate the drying. Paint the mass to make it more attractive.

Borax

Powdered borax, or hydrated sodium borate, is the

product that you will utilize most often. A drying agent, it will be useful in preserving the dead animals. Borax is economical because it can be used several times. It can be purchased in small quantities from your local drugstore.

For the heads of deer, caribou, and so forth, use borax in solution, mixed with alum and salt. The preparation of this solution will be described in Chapter 5.

CAUTION: Formerly taxidermists used a powder of arsenic — a dangerous poison that killed or sickened many of them. There is no danger in working with borax with your bare hands. However, *you must not eat any flesh that has been in direct contact with the borax.* Be sure to observe this precaution.

Your First Specimen

LET us suppose that you have acquired a golden woodpecker, or simply a pigeon. You will need the skin, the feathers, the wings, the feet, the tail, and the head.

Before you start to work, place all your tools and supplies within reach. Take care to spread some sheets of paper on your table or workbench, to collect unused borax. *A word of advice:* Never put your tools on the paper because you run the risk of forgetting them and inadvertently throwing them out with the paper.

SKINNING

Place the bird on your worktable on its back with the head at your left. Be sure to open the beak and fill it with padding. Then, without squeezing the beak too hard, bind it to keep it firmly closed. Pack the anus, to avoid all running of blood and excrement.

The Body

1. Separate the feathers from the hollow of the breast to the anus. Then take a scalpel (or, lacking that, a knife or a razor blade) and make an incision, without piercing the flesh, from the hollow of the breast to the anus. *You must do this carefully without pressing too hard, because there is no support in this region* (**Figure 3**).

2. Separate the skin at the right and at the left of the incision (**Figure 4**). Using the scissors or a knife, cut the tissues that do not separate easily.

Fig. 3. Making the incision. *Do not press too hard.*

Fig. 4. Separating the skin. Do not pull the skin.

3.   Next, cut the leg at the first joint (**Figure 5**).

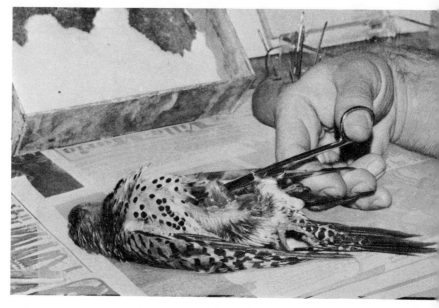

Fig. 5. Cutting the leg at the first joint.

4.   Without forcing it, separate the skin from the body with your fingers.

5.   If the skin is stuck too closely, continue with the scalpel, holding the skin in one hand and the instrument in the other. *Always be most careful not to pierce the skin.* Each useless cut that you make will only have to be sewed up later, and that will not always be easy.

Take your time. You will succeed. I am sure of it.

PRECAUTIONS. 'If you cut the flesh and some blood runs out, apply a little borax or Plaster of Paris, which will absorb the blood. If the breast feathers of the bird are white, you will try, without doubt, not to stain them. To prevent this, sew a piece of tissue or cardboard to the skin at each side of the incision. Thus, instead of holding the skin with your fingers you will be holding the cardboard. The cardboard or tissue is to be removed when you sew up the bird.

The Tail

1. Cut the end of the spine very carefully, leaving all the tail feathers attached.

2. With a pair of scissors, cut the little bone inside (**Figure 6**).

Fig. 6. Cutting the tail bone.

3. Continue to lift the skin from the back. Do this most carefully because the skin is very thin. If you try to proceed too quickly you run great risk of damaging your specimen.

The Wings

To prepare the wings you must first devote ten minutes to the making of an anchor. This will consist of three small chains, each of which ends in a fishhook. These three chains are connected by a ring to a pulley, fastened above your worktable.

1. Fix the fishhooks in the body of the bird (head down) and pull it as for a windlass (**Figure 7**).

Fig. 7. Suspending the specimen.
Do not let wing tips drag on the bench

*Do not let the tips of the wings
drag on the table while the bird is suspended, because they could be broken.*

2. With your bird thus suspended you will have
both hands free to continue removing the skin as far as
the wings.

3. Cut the wings with the scissors, near the body
(**Figure 8**).

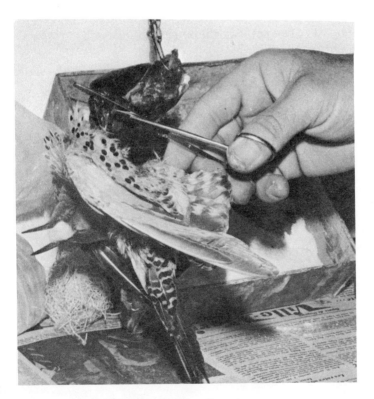

Fig. 8. Cutting the wings.

(Have you thought about changing your sheets of paper?)

The Head

The skin of the head is thinner than the rest. Therefore observe the following precautions:

1. Work as near as possible to the skull.

2. Take special care around the auditory passages and the eyelids.

3. Do not cut the eyelashes.

4. Do not puncture the eyeballs; the fluid would flood the feathers.

5. Lift up the skin as far as the beak without, however, detaching it completely (**Figure 9**).

Fig. 9. Lifting the skin without detaching it from the bill.

6. Now unhook the bird and place it on the table.

7. Cut the neck at the base of the skull (**Figure 10**).

Fig. 10. Cutting the neck at the base of the skull.

8. Put the body to one side; it will serve you during the mounting.

9. With the small pincers, enlarge the occipital hole, by which you will remove the brain. Do not leave any portion of the brain inside.

10. By the same opening, draw out the tongue and the palate.

11. Remove the eyes from the orbits. (If you have

not noted the color of the eyes, there is still time; even though the most propitious moment is always immediately after death.) The use of pieces of absorbent paper will facilitate this work of cleaning.

12. With the aid of a scalpel or a pair of scissors, remove the flesh from the top of the skull and from the skin of the neck, in order to avoid all future putrefaction. *Do this work rapidly* because the skin of these regions dries very quickly. This effect can be retarded by applying a damp cloth. Sprinkle it with some borax.

The skull of small birds has so little flesh that it is useless to build it up with modeling clay. (For larger birds, like the woodpecker, the flesh must be rebuilt with

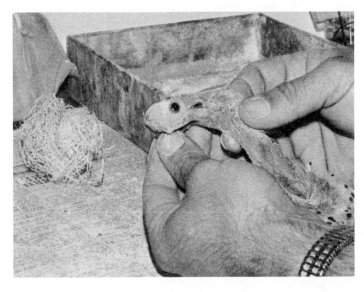

Fig. 11. Placing the artificial eyes and remodeling the skull if needed.

modeling clay, diluted with a little water to make it easier to handle.) Put clay in the orbits, however; but not too much (**Figure 11**). Remember that the stuffed bird must look as much as possible like a living one.

Replacing the Skin on the Skull

You are now ready to arrange the skin over the skull. To do this, push the skull gently with your thumbs, and with your index finger replace the skin over the skull. Put back the skin of the neck and then, holding the bird by the beak and shaking it vigorously, replace the wings and the feathers. For larger birds it is necessary to make a lengthwise cut below the neck in order to avoid tearing the skin. Make this incision big enough to permit taking out the skull and to allow for cleaning.

I regularly utilize the method of the old taxidermists in the Jardin des Plantes at Paris, who follow an ingenious procedure. They introduce a thread by the bird's nostrils and then they have only to pull it from the inside of the neck to replace the skin on the skull. Never force the skin of the neck in working it back. Cut it, rather, and resew it after the cleaning is finished.

The Feet

Now turn your attention to the feet, which you have not yet treated:

1. Turn back the skin and with a scalpel detach it as far as the second articulation, situated above the tarsal-metatarsal joint (**Figure 12**).

Fig. 12. Skinning the feet.

2. Repeat the operation on the other foot.

3. *Remove the remaining flesh*—do not neglect this (**Figure** 13).

Fig. 13. Removing the flesh from the feet.

4. Cut the end of the bone (**Figures 14, 15**).

5. Sprinkle the interior of the skin plentifully with borax, and do not omit that of the legs, or the bone.

6. Put the skin back around the bones of the legs.

Cleaning the Wings and Tail

To remove the flesh from the wings, make an incision along the bone. By feeling the latter, you can determine the length of the necessary incision. Draw out all the flesh with a cutting tool — the scalpel being the best. Then sprinkle this part plentifully with borax. Repeat the procedure on the other wing. It is not necessary to sew up these last incisions, unless the bird is very big or you wish to keep the wings spread open.

Concern yourself now with the tail. Remove the flesh still attached to the bony tip. Be most careful not to cut the tail feathers. Apply borax freely to this region. Your bird is now ready for mounting.

CAUTION. Let us note again that if the bird is a pheasant, a duck, or any other animal of which you wish to eat the flesh, instead of borax to absorb the blood or other fluid, you should use corn meal. But, above all, do not eat any flesh that has been in direct contact with borax.

STUFFING

For the work of stuffing you need some galvanized wires of different sizes, such as the following:

Fig. 14. Cutting the end of the leg bone (a).

Fig. 15. Cutting the end of the leg bone (b).

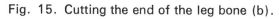

No. 9 or 10: For falcons, hawks, gos-
              hawks, marsh buzzards,
              ducks, black ducks.

No. 12 or 14: For gulls, large wood-
              peckers, kingfishers.

No. 16 or 18: For starlings, bluejays,
              blackbirds.

Note that the higher the number, the finer the wire. Never use a wire that is too fine because your animal will be wobbly after it is mounted.

You should have at hand a variety of artificial eyes. It is very important to use eyes of the same size and color as those in the living animal, because if there is one thing that is remarked in a stuffed animal, it is the eyes.

Construction of the Form

The stripped skin of the bird is on your worktable. You must now make an artificial body, which, in taxidermy is called a *form*.

The fault of all beginners, without exception, is making forms that are too big. To prevent this, measure the body of the bird very carefully, noting length, diameter, and other measurements. Take a handful of straw and sprinkle it with water — not too much. Wind nylon thread around the straw without squeezing it too hard (**Figure 16**). Compare it with the model (**Figure 17**).

If it seems too small, add some straw and continue

Fig. 16. Preparing the form (a).

Fig. 17. Preparing the form (b).

to wind it with the thread without undoing what you did first.

Remember that the form should never in any case be bigger than the body. It is easy, if the form is slightly smaller, to adjust it with some wadding during the mounting. Make a test: put the form within the skin and see whether you can bring the two sides of the skin together for the purpose of sewing them (**Figure 18**). If you can, your form has been well made.

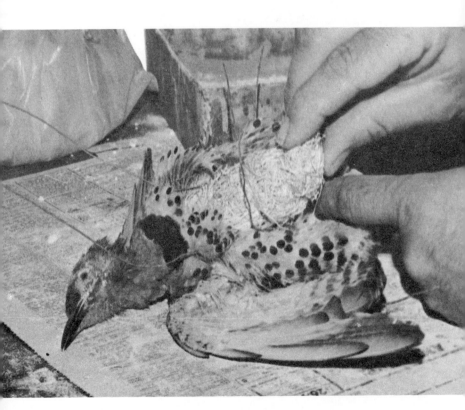

Fig. 18. Adjusting the form.

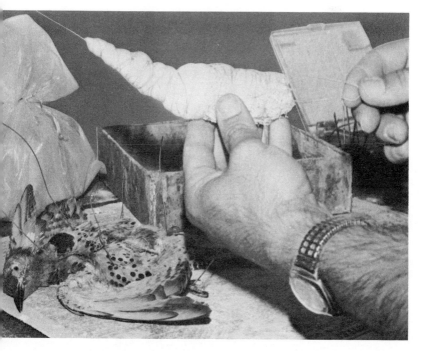

Fig. 19. Inserting the stem.

Mounting the Head

Measure the length of the skin from head to tail and add five inches. Cut a wire of this length. Bend one end of it in the form of a *U*, calculating that the other end should extend a few inches beyond the head. Pass this through the form so that the *U* is at the tail. This will prevent the stem from moving inside the form (**Figure 19**).

At the neck cover the other end of the wire with padding, diminishing the thickness near the head. Tie it without squeezing it too hard; the neck should retain

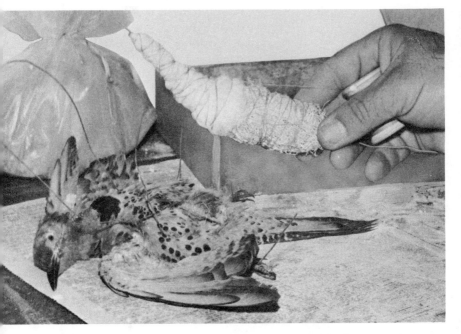

Fig. 20. Forming the neck.

a certain flexibility (**Figure 20**).

At the beginning, one has a tendency to make necks too long. Now the necks of birds, with the exception of such creatures as geese, ospreys, and herons, are short; thus it is important to observe the living bird well and to know its habits. A duck, for example, has a very short neck when it is on the water, but it becomes longer in flight.

You must now introduce into the skull the end of the stem that passes through the form. To do this, push the form firmly toward the base of the skull so that the neck fits properly. Leave the part of the stem that extends beyond the head until the bird is completely dry — that is, until about 12 days after the end of the stuffing. Certain taxidermists prefer to take out the stem by the beak, rather than by the skull; this is a matter of personal preference.

Mounting the Feet

Measure the length of the legs, from the inside to the bottom of the feet, and add 8 inches. Cut two stems of wire of this length. File them to a tip, which will facilitate introducing them into the feet. Take one of these stems, insert it into the bottom of the foot, and slide it along the bone, passing behind the joint (**Figure 21**).

Fig. 21. Inserting the stem in the foot.

Perform this operation slowly, but with a sure hand and with the fewest possible thrusts. If the stem bends, withdraw it and start over again. When it reaches the inside, stop pushing and draw it with your fingers. Allow a few inches to extend beyond the foot, however, which will permit attaching the bird to its stand.

Fasten together the bone of the leg and the stem with thread, always without squeezing too hard (**Figure 22**).

Then take some padding and put it around in place of the flesh of the legs. Be careful not to use too much;

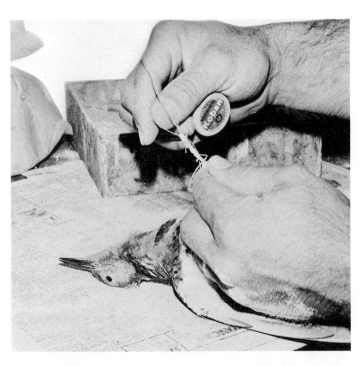

Fig. 22. Fastening the stem to the bone.

you should be able to draw the skin down without stretching it. Keep the padding in place by winding thread around it (**Figure 23**).

Fig. 23. Placing the padding.

With larger birds, because the skin is thicker, it is more difficult to put the stems of the legs in place, even though they are pointed. Generally, one makes an incision with a scalpel under the feet before inserting the stems.

Once the form is in place inside the skin, attach

43

the stems of the legs to it, taking great care that they enter the form at good spots. Final success will depend largely on this provision. It is to facilitate this work that one divides the bone of the legs.

You must have decided already on the definitive position in which you wish to place your specimen. To facilitate the introduction of the stems from the feet through the form, you can make two holes in the form with the aid of a knitting needle; the diameter should be the same as that of the stem. The use of too big a knitting needle would cause loose articulation of the form. When the stem has gone through the form, bend the end of it into a U. Then draw on the part of the stem that extends beyond the bottom of the foot until the latter is well secured.

Fig. 24. The specimen in place.

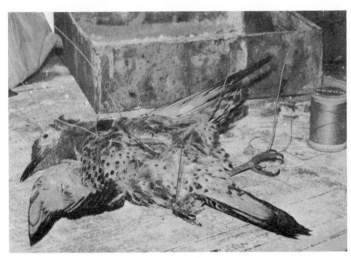

Fig. 25. Distributing the padding.

Sewing the Incision

The complete form is in place. The legs of the bird are set up and placed near the body (**Figure 24**).

Check that you can close the skin over the form without too much squeezing, and that there is no empty space inside. This is often found around the neck, the legs, the wings, and the tail. With the tweezer, fill any space with padding, and be careful to distribute it well. See that the skin is not stretched too much (**Figure 25**).

Thread your needle and start to sew up the inci-

45

sion at the neck; be sure you knot the thread securely (**Figure 26**).

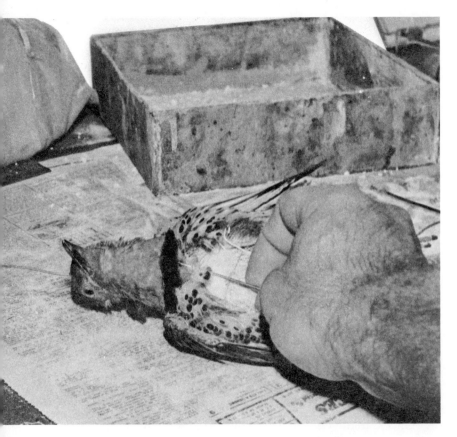

Fig. 26. The beginning.

Continue from left to right, passing the needle under the skin (**Figure 27**).

Replace the feathers after each stitch in order to

Fig. 27. Sewing the incision.

hide the seam (**Figure 28**).

Be careful that the thread does not coil itself around the feathers; that would give the bird a very bad appearance.

Fig. 28. The completed incision.

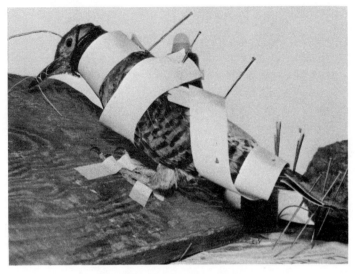

Fig. 29. The temporary base.

MOUNTING

Attaching to Temporary Base

For the duration of the drying period, attach the bird to a temporary base (as in **Figure 29**).

Use a branch or a plank, according to your choice of the definitive position of the animal. Our golden woodpecker has a plank for a base because, once it is dry, it will rest on a flat pedestal. Do not throw out these temporary bases; they can be used again.

Be most careful, because the position set on the temporary base should be scrupulously the same as the position it must have on the permanent base. *Once dry, in fact, to change the position would mean breaking the bones of the bird.*

Refresh your memory of the various attitudes of the living animal. Then proceed calmly and surely, without any brusque movement. Using the stem that passes through the skull, place the head in the desired position. Patience, and a critical and artistic eye, will allow you to practice your gifts of observation and your knowledge of zoology.

Take a drill or other device. Be sure that the borer is the size of the stems that pass through the feet. Make two holes through the stand, corresponding to the separation chosen for the feet.

Insert the stems of the feet in the holes. Wrap the excess around the temporary base so that it will do no harm during the drying of the feet. Secure the feet to the base with little pins. If the feet are already too dry, keep them moist with a damp cloth for a few hours, until you can safely work on them.

Placing the Wings

Do not adjust the wings until the animal is on the temporary base. Check the position of the feathers, very carefully and one by one. Set the wings by means of pins about two inches long. Place the first pin in the upper part of the wing — that is, at the height of the bone nearest to the body. Check the solidity of the whole assemblage.

If the wing moves, start over again a little higher or a little lower; there should be a certain resistance. On small birds one pin should be enough for a wing. Use pins of stainless steel, which will not corrode in contact with the chemical products employed. Rusty pins would easily break and the wings of your bird would be displaced.

Placing the Tail

Measure the length of the tail and add three inches. Cut a stem of this length. Bend one end of it into the shape of a T and sharpen the other end. Insert the stem into the anus until the bar of the T is completely hidden under the tail feathers, because this permanent support for the tail must be invisible.

Cut two pieces of cardboard (such as one finds in shirts returned by the laundry), fairly wide but not too long. Place one of these under the tail, the other above it (**Figure 30**).

Fig. 30. Placing the tail.

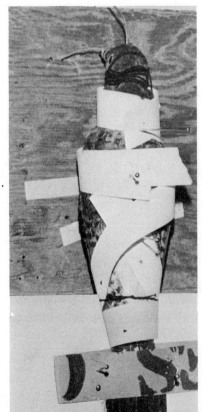

Lightly separate the tail feathers; not too much — this is their position at rest. (In flight, the tail feathers, like the wings, are fully open; the bird draws them in when it wishes to land.) Pin, or rather, hook the two pieces of cardboard together. Assure yourself that the feathers are well placed, because this is the position that they will have when they are dry.

Placing the Eyes

The method I prefer consists of placing the eyes before pulling the skin from the skull, while the eyelids are still moist (see **Figure 11**). If, however, you do not have the artificial eyes at that moment, place a bit of padding between the eyelids so that they will not close in drying.

As soon as you have the eyes, put them in place, after removing the padding and separating the eyelids, with the aid of a damp cloth in order not to damage them. Check whether there is sufficient modeling clay in the orbits. If there is too much take some out, a little at a time.

Cut to a good length the stem that holds the eye. Push it down into the center of the orbit until you can pull down the eyelid. Delicately raise the latter, with the aid of a knitting needle, a tweezer, or any other instrument that will not damage this very fragile skin. Do not use eyes that are too large; your bird would look stupid. And do not use eyes that stand out from the head; that would not be pretty.

A *trick:* Put a little cement or wood glue in the orbit and behind the eye. The eyes will remain well attached; but do not proceed until you have found the

51

right position.

If during your work you find that the eyelids dry too quickly, moisten them with a damp cloth.

Preparation for Drying

With your tweezer, fill the throat of the bird through the beak with small pieces of wadding, being very careful that this does not form a ball. When you judge that you have used enough, shape the throat from the outside by pressing the wadding. The throat must be well filled out.

Unless in the final position the bird's beak is to be open, it is necessary, for greater solidity, to close it by puncturing the two parts, from underneath and toward the throat, with a pin. Another procedure is to pass a needleful of thread through the nostrils of the bird and make a few turns of it around the beak, ending with a double knot (see **Figure 29**). You will cut away the thread after the drying. If you omit this step, the bird's beak will remain open during the drying and you will then have to glue it shut and run the risk of breaking it.

While the bird still shows a certain flexibility, assure yourself that all the wing feathers and tail feathers are in correct position. Blow on the plumage, or use a knitting needle to replace a feather that is out of order. For the feathers surrounding the eye, insert the large end of a knitting needle under the eyelid and gently raise the skin. The feathers will fall into place.

To avoid displacement of the feathers during drying wrap the bird in little strips of paper or woolen thread; the latter gives excellent results around the head. Squeeze just enough to keep the feathers in place, because if you squeeze too hard, marks will appear on the plumage. Use pins to hold the strips of paper (see **Figure 29**). Adopt the good habit of writing the date on one of these strips (**Figure 31**).

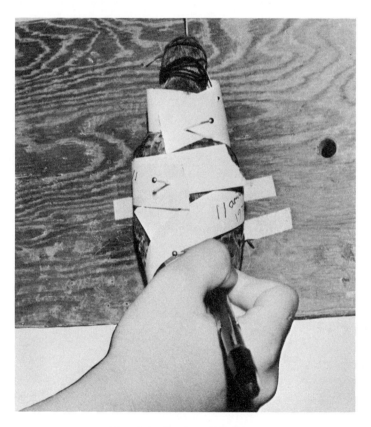

Fig. 31. Dating the strips.

The bird is ready. The duration of the drying is proportional to the size of the specimen. For little birds, this varies between 10 and 14 days.

Examine your stuffed specimen every day. This daily inspection will permit you to verify that the drying is proceeding normally. If the wool or the strips of paper slip, replace them. If the eyelids are closing during the drying, keep them open by sticking in a few pins; but be careful not to displace the eyes if they are already in position.

Restoring Colors

Your bird is completely dry. Aided by your photographs and memories, paint the beak and the feet. Use the best quality of oil paint in a tube, which you will dilute with a few drops of boiled linseed oil. (CAUTION: Do not boil this yourself.) Its function is to liquefy the paint without changing the color. Do not prepare too much at one time; you need so little of it.

To obtain the desired color, you may have to make a mixture. Here is a short table of colors that you can obtain by mixing:

GRAY = Zinc white + dark cadmium yellow
ORANGE = Light cadmium yellow + red + light vermilion
FLESH = Zinc white + light vermilion + yellow ochre

You will soon become familiar with these mixtures and you will know how to obtain your desired color without fumbling.

Allow the paint to dry and then remove the woolen binding and paper strips.

Certain taxidermists simply varnish the feet and beak of a stuffed bird. I prefer the results I obtain with the use of paint.

Completion

Cut the stem that passes through the skull. So as not to spoil the feathers of the head, here is a very simple trick: Pierce a hole in the center of a piece of stiff cardboard and run this onto the stem. Hold the cardboard against the head with one hand and with the other cut off with a nipper the end of the stem that sticks out.

Do not cut off the support of the tail feathers; just see that it is well hidden under the feathers.

Examine the periphery of the eyes, especially the corners of the eyelids. If there are any open spaces, plug them with some beeswax, which you can melt in a teaspoon over a candle. Because this wax cools very quickly, apply it rapidly with a little stick.

Put your bird on its definitive base — a branch, or any other support of your choice. If it is of wood, coat the stems with cement or wood glue before inserting them in the holes in the base.

You can now submit your masterpiece to the critics. If one should find any faults, remember that "Perfection is not of this world, but one must constantly strive to attain it" (**Figure 32**).

Fig. 32.
The completed specimen.

STUFFING A BIRD WITH WINGS SPREAD

The stuffing of a bird with its wings spread is not particularly difficult, but it presents certain problems for a beginner. Before tackling them he should work with a few birds that have closed wings. The beginner must also acquire some knowledge of the attitudes and habits of the living bird and a certain mastery of taxidermy.

To illustrate this manner of stuffing I have chosen a common loon. But it could just as well be a partridge, a goose, a wild goose, a bluejay, a golden woodpecker, or a thrush.

In many steps the process of stuffing is the same as just described. I shall note only the differences.

Skin the bird as usual, but when you reach the head make an incision on the top of the skull, just below the curve, separating the feathers well so that they will be cut as little as possible. If the bird has a crest, make the incision in the throat.

With a scalpel, loosen the skin near the neck as far as its base. When removing the head, enlarge the incision rather than tear the skin. As usual, cut the neck near the base of the skull, and through this hole remove the brain, the tongue, and bits of flesh with a tweezer. Sprinkle the skull and the inside of the neck with borax. Sew up the incision immediately; the seam should be invisible.

Cut the center of the bottom of the wing with a scalpel, take away the flesh of the upper arm and forearm, and scrape the bones with a little knife. Sprinkle with borax. Measure the total length of the wing and add five inches.

Cut a strong stem and insert this from underneath along the bone of the wing. The stem is in proper place when it holds the wing outspread. Proceed in the same manner with the other wing, and place the form within the skin.

If necessary, consult some books and photographs before you set the wings in their definitive position. Hook or pin a piece of heavy cardboard under the wings — or a galvanized wire, depending on the size of the bird — which will hold them in the chosen curve during the drying (**Figures 33, 33A**).

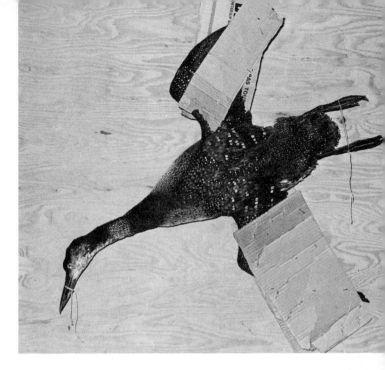

Fig. 33-33A. Spreading the wings.

If you should wish to hang your bird on the wall, measure the width of the body and add two inches. Cut two stems of this length. Make a point at one end and a loop at the other end of each. Push the two stems in on both sides of the center of gravity and about four inches apart. Cross the body from one side to the other and bend back the sharpened ends. Pass a brass wire through the two loops; your anchor is ready. Use it to suspend the animal during drying (**Figure 34**).

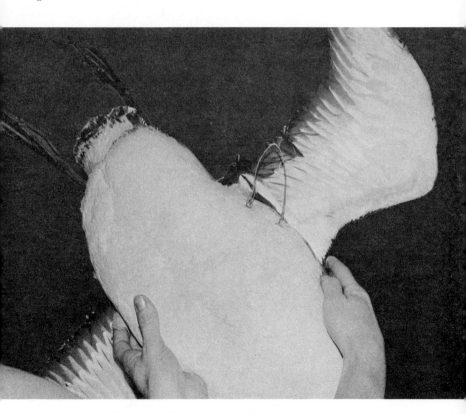

Fig. 34. Placing the anchor.

Fig. 35. A common loon.

Mammals

THE fur of animals that are killed must be treated with the greatest of care, especially in the hot season. Whatever kind of animal is used, start by plugging with wadding every opening by which blood or excrement could escape: mouth, nostrils, anus, open wounds, or holes from bullets or shot. Wipe the fur at once to remove every trace of blood, which should not in any case have time to dry. Comb the fur in the right direction and put the animal into a bag for transporting it.

If you kill an animal during the hot season and you will not be returning home the same day, skin it on the spot and apply a generous layer of table salt to the entire surface of the skin. This is not necessary during the winter because the cold will preserve it perfectly as far as its destination, on the express condition that there is no contact with any source of heat. When you skin an animal in the woods keep the skull, after removing the brain, the eyes, and the tongue.

The stuffing of a gray squirrel will serve to illustrate my explanations; but it could have been a red one, which is very easily found in our forests; or a black one, which is a very beautiful specimen. If you do not have an animal of your own, buy a small living rabbit at the market.

SKINNING

Assure yourself that the squirrel is cold enough, so that the blood will be well coagulated. Check that your tools are ready. Place the animal on the worktable with the head at your left. Measure the length from the head to the base of the tail, and add five inches. Cut a stem of this length, of No. 12 or No. 13 wire; we shall call this the principal stem.

The Body

1. Pack the mouth and anus with wadding and spread the feet wide apart (**Figure 36**).

2. Separate the fur with your fingers so as to cut the fewest possible hairs.

3. With a scalpel open a linear incision from the

Fig. 36. Packing the openings.

abdomen to the anus, which you go around (**Figure 37**).

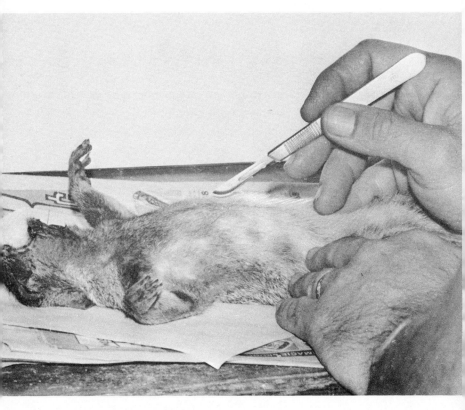

Fig. 37. Making the incision.

4. Lift up the skin as far as the hind legs (**Figure 38**) and push the leg toward the inside, so as to release the thigh (**Figure 39**).

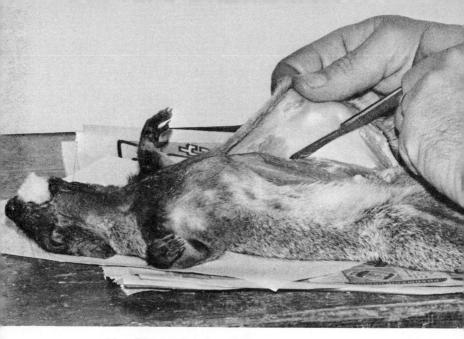

Fig. 38. Lifting the skin.

Fig. 39. Releasing the thigh.

5. Cut the bone near the body (**Figure 40**). If a little blood escapes, apply some borax.

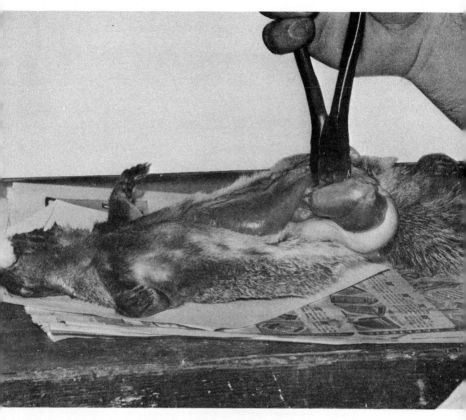

Fig. 40. Cutting the bone near the body.

6. Separate the fur to the ends of the legs, but do not cut the feet (**Figure 41**).

7. Separate the skin from the nerve of the tail,

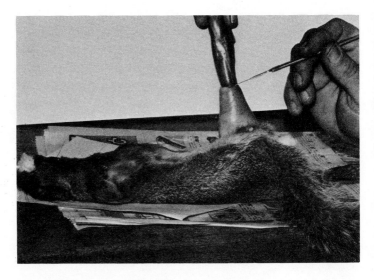

Fig. 41. Separating the fur.

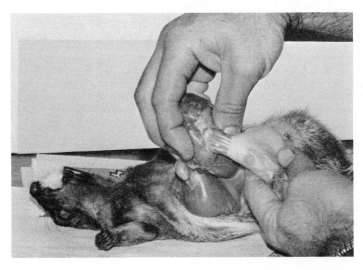

Fig. 42. Separating the skin from the tail nerve.

for about three inches (**Figure 42**).

8. Take the skin in one hand, the nerve in the other (**Figure 43**), and pull firmly and smoothly until you have loosened the nerve completely (**Figure 44**).

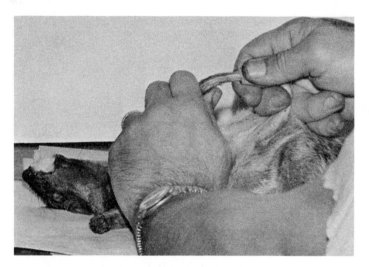

Fig. 43. Removing the tail nerve (a).

Fig. 44. Removing the tail nerve (b).

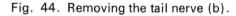

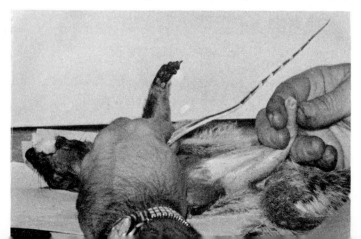

Fig. 45. Cutting the leg bone near the body.

9. If, by mischance, you break the nerve, cut the exterior of the skin from below in order to draw out the whole nerve. Do not forget the least bit of it, because the drying that it would cause would make the tail fall after a few months.

For the muskrat, you cut the tail throughout its full length in order to withdraw the nerve.

10. Hang the body of the squirrel, head down, on the anchor (as explained in preceding chapter).

11. Loosen the fur as far as the front legs, and cut the bone at the first joint (**Figure 45**).

12. Continue skinning the body (**Figures 46–47**).

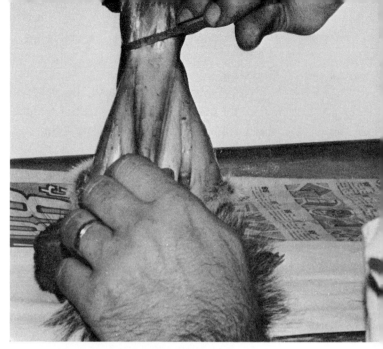

Fig. 46. Separating the skin from the body.

Fig. 47. Separating the skin near the head.

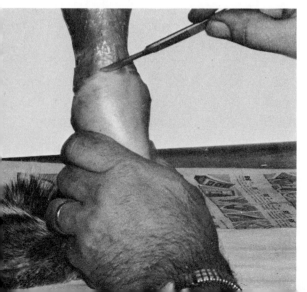

The Head

Here you are at the head. Be very careful not to make any inadvertent cuts with the scalpel in the skin, which you would have to sew up later.

1. Proceed slowly as far as the ears, which you cut near the auditory passage (**Figure 48**).

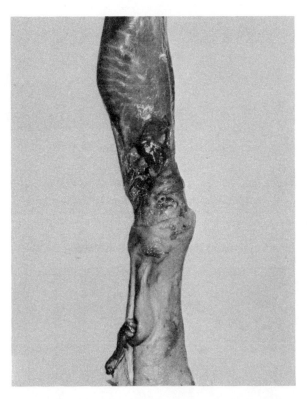

Fig. 48. The ears. The skin is cut very near the auditory passage.

2. When you come to the eyes (which are covered by the folded skin), cut delicately around the orbit (**Figure 49**).

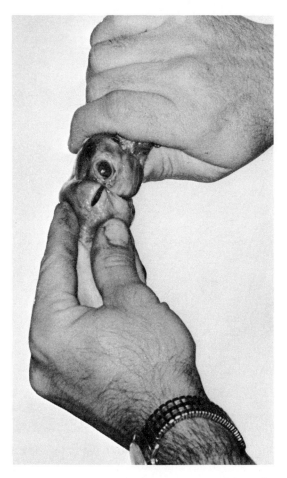

Fig. 49. The eyes. Great care should be taken not to cut the eyelids.

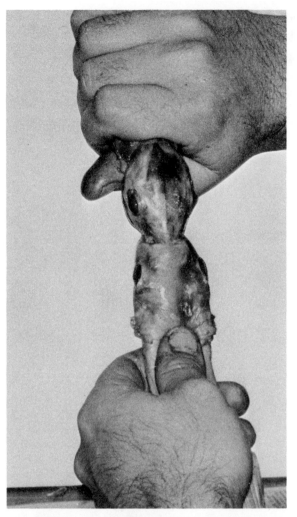

Fig. 50. The nose does not have to be separated
from the skull.

3. Continue as far as the end of the nose, without cutting the cartilage (**Figure 50**).

72

4. Unhook the animal and cut through the neck at the base of the skull (**Figure 51**).

Fig. 51. Cutting the neck at the base of the skull.

5. Empty the skull, lift out the eyes and the tongue, and remove every morsel of flesh (**Figures 52, 53, 54**).

Fig. 52. Emptying the skull.

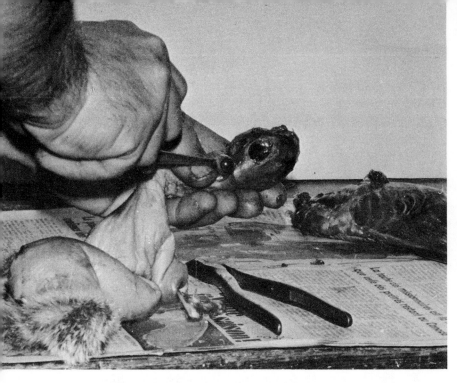

Fig. 53. Removing the eyes.

Fig. 54. Cleaning the skull again.

CLEANING THE SKIN

1. Scrape the entire inside of the skin.

2. Make a small incision under the legs, take out as much flesh as possible, and sprinkle with borax.

3. Cut along the full length of the tail (**Figures 55–56**).

Fig. 55. Cutting full length of tail.

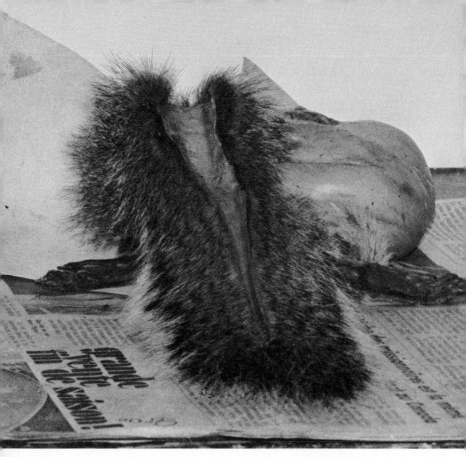

Fig. 56. Tail skin wide open.

4. Now spread the skin out on your table and apply a light layer of salt to the whole surface; make it penetrate by rubbing it hard. Then apply a second layer of salt, but do not rub it (**Figure 57**).

5. Wet a clean cloth, cover the entire skin with it, and leave it overnight (**Figure 58**).

Fig. 57. Salting the skin.

Fig. 58. Covering the skin.

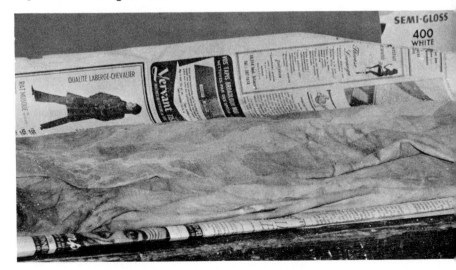

6. The next day, prepare in a sink or basin a cold soapy solution, using a detergent of the kind used for washing linens.

7. Wash the skin, several times if necessary, until every trace of blood has disappeared. Rinse carefully in cold water to remove the soap. For these two operations, *never use hot or tepid water;* that is the secret of success.

8. Hang up the skin and press it with your hands, without twisting it. Let it hang until it is completely drained.

Certain taxidermists neither salt nor wash their skins in the manner described here. I have obtained astonishing results with this method, and the animal always retains a very beautiful fur coat from which the hairs never fall.

If you do not have the time to stuff your squirrel immediately, cover the inside of the skin with a layer of salt and wrap it in a very damp cloth. You will have to check and, if necessary, renew the damp cloth every day, but you need not renew the salt. This dampness will keep all the suppleness in the skin indefinitely. When you do decide to stuff it, you will have to rinse the skin very carefully, to get rid of every trace of salt.

STUFFING

Making the Form
Take all the measurements that you will judge to

be useful in making the form. You can even trace the outline of the body on brown paper. This measuring is not superfluous work, but a good habit to have, because your eye is not always sufficient. Take the principal stem, which you have already prepared, and cover it with a good layer of paste. Roll up a little straw and tie it solidly (**Figure 59**). Gradually add more straw, tying it each time. Continue this until the form looks as much as possible like the body (**Figure 60**).

Fig. 59. Preparing the form (a).

Fig. 60. Preparing the form (b).

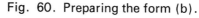

Another way of proceeding is to make the form first and then pass the stem through it.

Mounting the Tail

Measure the tail and add eight inches (**Figure 61**).

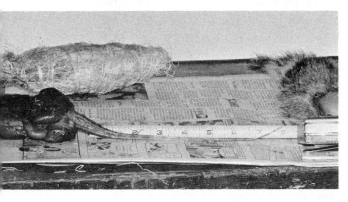

Fig. 61.
Measuring the tail.

Cut a stem of this length and roll it in padding; this takes the place of the nerve (**Figure 62**). The bit of stem that extends out will serve to fasten the tail to the form.

Fig. 62.
The tail padding.

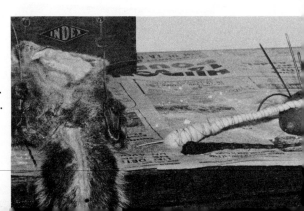

Mounting the Head

Substitute modeling clay for the flesh that you have removed. If the clay is too dry, moisten your fingers and work it into the skull itself. Do not forget the orbits. You can place the artificial eyes now but you will always be able to place them after you have finished the stuffing (**Figure 63**). Then draw the skin over the head (**Figure 64**).

Fig. 63. Placing the artificial eyes.

Fig. 64. Replacing the head skin.

Mounting the Legs

Measure the legs, add five inches, and cut some stems of this length. Make these finer than the principal stem. Note that the four legs are not of the same length. Insert the leg stem from below and slide it along the bone (**Figure 65**).

Tie the leg stem, and roll wadding around it, which you secure with thread (**Figures 66–67**).

Fig. 65. Inserting the leg stem.

Fig. 66. Tying the leg stem.

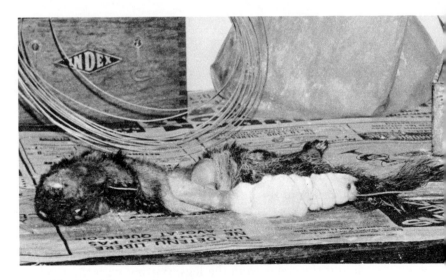

Fig. 67. Wadding the leg stem.

Then smooth down the skin, which should be done without difficulty, in order to check that the leg is of the right size. Repeat the operation on the three other legs and feet (**Figure 68**).

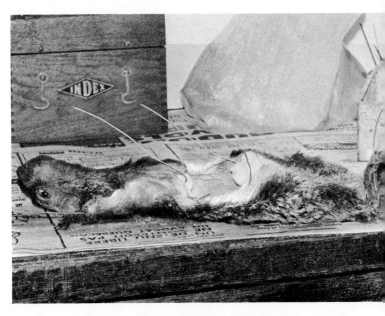

Fig. 68. Trying the skin over the leg.

Now apply a good layer of borax to the inside of the skin and try it on the form. Let the central stem emerge from the nose or the skull of the squirrel. Check carefully whether the two sides of the skin meet correctly, with just a little pulling.

Withdraw only the rear end of the form and push into it the stems from the legs, starting with the forelegs (**Figures 69 and 70**).

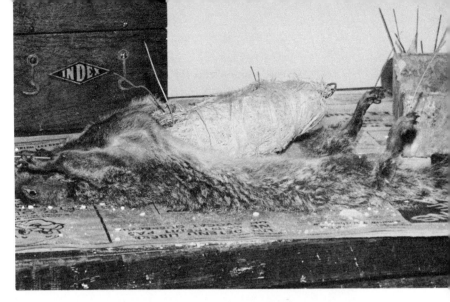

Fig. 69. Inserting the leg stems in the form (a).

Fig. 70. Inserting the leg stems in the form (b).

Secure the stems well by drawing them toward the inside with a pincers. Attach them two by two, very firmly by twisting them with the pincers (**Figure 71**).

Fig. 71. Attaching the leg stems.

The excess should be cut off (**Figure 72**).

Fold the end within the form in order to avoid harming the skin. A few inches of stem should always extend beyond the bottoms of the feet.

Securing the Tail

Make a loop in the part of the principal stem that

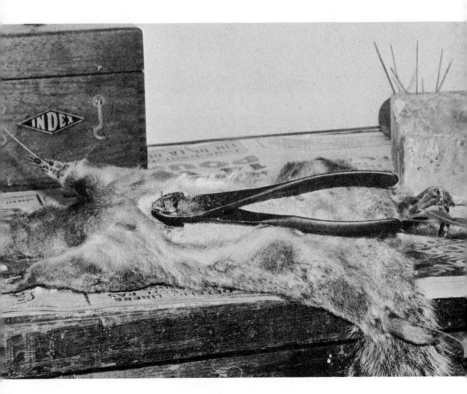

Fig. 72. Cutting the excess stem.

Fig. 73. Attaching the tail.

passes by the anus. Attach the end of the tail firmly to this (**Figure 73**).

Sewing the Incisions

Sew up the incision in the tail, starting at the end. Be very careful to put the hairs back in place after every stitch. Stop your sewing at the anus by passing your needle through several times from left to right, and end with a firm knot (**Figure 74**).

Fig. 74. Sewing the incision.

Cut off the excess of stem that extends beyond the nose, making a slight bend in it in order to cut as close as possible; one should not be able to see any trace of it (**Figure 75**).

Fig. 75. Cutting the stem at the nose.

Sew up the incision with very strong nonputrefying nylon thread (of the kind used for fishing). Start at the top of the abdomen, going from left to right, spacing the stitches half an inch apart. Do not forget to replace the hairs properly after each stitch. When you

Fig. 76. The seam.

come to the anus, pass the needle and thread several times over the same spot, and end with a knot. The seam should be invisible (**Figure 76**).

MOUNTING

Attaching to Base

To place the squirrel on a temporary base pierce four holes in the base, of the same size as the stems of the legs. Insert the stems in the holes. Do not place the legs too far apart. The animal should look as much as possible as if it were alive, perhaps with the tail in the arc of a circle, the back slightly arched, a nut in the mouth or between the paws. Use your imagination, memories, photographs, books, and so on (**Figure 77**).

91

Preparation for Drying

The modeling clay in the skull is not yet dry. Take advantage of this to correct, if necessary, the position of the eyes. With the large end of a needle, go around the periphery of the eyes. If the animal is to have the mouth closed, push a pin in below the jaws (you will remove this after the specimen is dry). If you are going to use a nut, place it between the teeth before you put in the pin. You can also prepare an artificial tongue of papier-mâché

The teeth of a squirrel are generally yellowed. If you wish to whiten them, rub them with a swab of

Fig. 77. The temporary base.

Fig. 78. Pinning the ears.

cotton on a little stick wet with hydrochloric (muriatic) acid. *Do not leave the acid on more than five or six seconds,* because if it comes in contact with the gums, you run the risk of having the teeth fall out after a short time. Wipe the acid away with another cotton swab wet with water. Repeat this operation several times if necessary; this method is good for all animals.

Plug the ears with some modeling paste or plasticine, so that they will remain in place during the drying. On one side of the base plant a long pine, and for the other side cut a little piece of cardboard, which you will pin along the ear so that it will not bend (**Figure 78**).

Pin each toe to the base, or hold it down with a band of gummed cloth tape. Plant a pin at the center of each foot (**as in Figure 78**).

Using a brush with soft hairs, brush the fur carefully, everywhere, and in both directions, except the tail, which you brush only once, against the direction of growth.

Allow the squirrel to dry for at least ten days in a dry place such as a garage or a cellar. Write the date

Fig. 79. The completed specimen.

of the stuffing on a piece of paper and affix it to the base.

Examine your animal every day and make any adjustments that may be necessary.

Completion

When the squirrel is dry, take away the pins and cardboard, and clean out the ears. Mix some oil paint (from a tube) the color of lampblack, with a little boiled linseed oil, and with a very good brush retouch the end of the nose, the lips, and the periphery of the eyes.

Place the animal on its permanent base — a branch or a pedestal. Brush the fur one last time. Your master-piece is finished. Show it to your friends, and accept their criticism (**Figure 79**).

Treatment of Skins

THE fresh skin of a deer, an elk, a wolf, a lynx, a fox, or similar animals, can be preserved as follows:

After skinning the animal, assure yourself that you have left absolutely no morsel of flesh on the skin (**Figure 80**) and that you have completely removed the nerve from the tail (**Figure 81**).

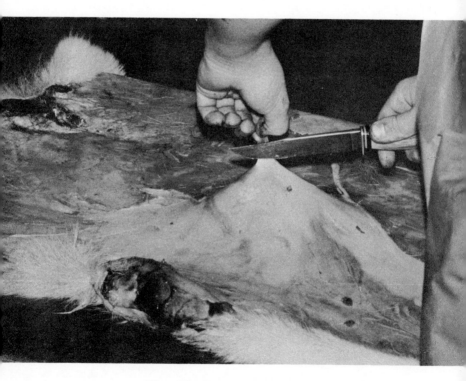

Fig. 80. Removing the flesh from the skin.

Fig. 81. Removing the nerve from the tail.

SALTING

Spread the skin out as much as you can (**Figure 82**). Carefully apply a generous layer of table salt to the inside. Rub every bit of skin energetically and let it rest for an hour so that the salt will absorb as much blood as possible. Then apply a second layer of salt on top of the first. Do not be stingy because wherever you do not salt the skin the hair will fall out.

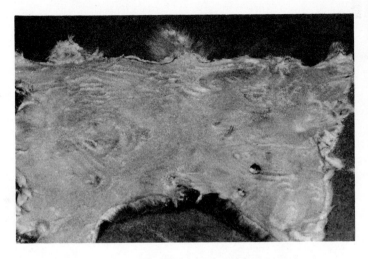

Fig. 82. Salting the skin.

Roll the skin with the hairs inside and put it away in a dry place (**Figure 83**). At least three days of rest are necessary before starting to work on the skin.

If you cannot work on the skin after this lapse of time, unroll it and remove the reddened salt and shreds of flesh. Resalt it more moderately, roll it up, and put it away again in a dry place. A skin so prepared can wait indefinitely until you have time to work on it.

When you are ready, remove the salt by rinsing the skin in clear cold water. Then prepare some cold soapy water with a customary household detergent, in a sink, bathtub, or washing machine; do not turn the

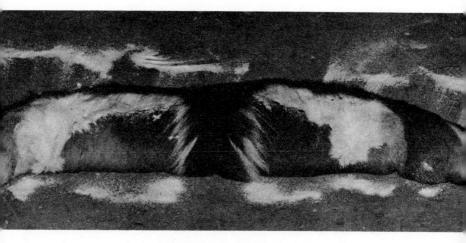

Fig. 83. Rolling the skin.

washing machine on. Wash the skin several times if necessary until every trace of blood or saltiness has disappeared. Rinse in cold water.

The skin is now ready to go to the tannery — unless you should wish to tan it yourself, which is a little more complicated and requires much work. You will probably want to use the tannery unless the skin that you offer is not accepted.

TANNING

Preparing the Solution

Bring one gallon of water to a boil. Stir in the following ingredients until they dissolve: three pounds of table salt, one-half pound of alum, and one-half pound of powdered borax. Add four gallons of water. Allow the mixture to cool. This solution can be used several times — until it gives off a nauseous odor.

Immersion

Pour the solution into a receptacle of wood, nylon, plastic or glass — but *never of metal*. Totally immerse the skin that you have just washed, pushing it down with a stick if necessary. Stir it every other day, checking carefully whether the immersion of the skin is complete. At the end of twelve days for the skin of a deer (longer for a larger skin), take the skin out of the vessel and allow it to drain above it. For this purpose place a stick across the vessel.

Then reexamine the skin minutely, because it could hold some blood spots — for example, around the holes made by shot. If necessary, brush the hair at these places with a small metal brush. Sew up the holes, after first giving them an oval shape in order to bring the edges together properly.

Wash the skin again in cold soapy water, several times if necessary. Rinse it for ten minutes in cold water. Spread the skin and nail it all around to a wooden panel. Using a good knife, remove all bits of flesh that remain on the skin. Hold the knife in both hands.*

Stretching

Next remove the nails and stretch the skin until it becomes supple and dry. Get some friends to help you because this work takes eight to ten hours. The more you stretch the skin, the more supple it will

* You may also use a butcher's chopper, or a plane—or better still, a paintscraper; make the corners of the scraper round so as not to damage the skin. A special knife is available from taxidermy suppliers.

become. If you have to stop momentarily before the end of the operation, wrap the skin completely in a large damp cloth that will keep it from drying. If you have to stop for a long time, plunge the skin back into the tanning solution; but *do not forget to stretch it during the drying.*

If you have no assistance, you must proceed differently. After the scraping, remove the nails from the skin and turn it over. This time the hairs are on top. Hook or nail the skin at its center, following the line of the back. Space the hooks or nails at one-inch intervals and do not drive them too deep, so that the hairs will not be pulled out when you remove the nails from the skin.

Next take one side of the skin and pull it as hard as possible. Without loosening your hold, nail the skin to an inch of the board. Do not be stingy with the nails because the skin has a great tendency to shrink in drying. Repeat the operation with the other side.

When the skin is completely dry, sand it, just as you would a surface of wood, starting from the center. This method is shorter than the preceding, and it also gives excellent results. The nails must be rustproof.

Here is still another procedure: Take a piece of wood with rounded corners and place it in a vise. Rub the skin on the wood.

The skin is now tanned. Now you must cut it to make it symmetrical. Do not use a pair of scissors for this, but a scalpel or a very sharp knife. Cut the skin on the leather side. See the finished skins in **Figures 84** and **84A.**

Fig. 84. The finished skin
(not cut symmetrically).

REMOVING HAIRS FROM A SKIN

After rinsing the skin to remove the salt, wash it
in cold water. You can use a washing machine with a
household detergent, and it does not matter if the skin
loses some hairs there. Then put it into a non-metallic
vessel, containing three gallons of cold water and one
pint of lime. Let it soak for 24 to 48 hours — until the
hairs begin to loosen. Check the skin often and do not

allow it to remain beyond this length of time. Rinse in cold water and remove the hairs with, for example, a little hoe. Then stretch the skin until it is completely dry; or nail it to a panel.

If you have to interrupt your work for any length of time before the end of this operation, put the skin into the tanning solution, which will preserve it indefinitely.

Fig. 84A. The finished skin.

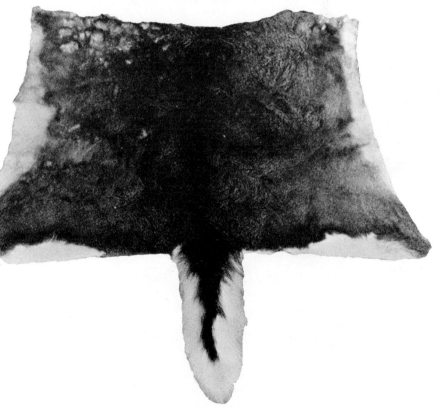

Mounting the Head of a Deer

WHAT hunter has not dreamed of stuffing a stag's head? The head of this magnificent animal of the deer family makes a splendid trophy, especially when it has antlers. When you have gained sufficient experience in taxidermy, you can start on any animal at your disposition, young male or female.

In this chapter, we shall mount the head of a young female deer, without horns. The work is identical in the case of a head with horns.

Fig. 85.
Area of cut for
head with antlers.

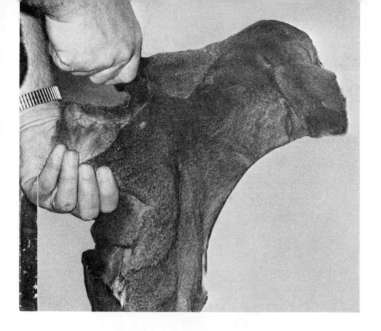

Fig. 86. Starting the incision.

CUTTING OFF THE HEAD

Four hours are necessary for skinning the head of a deer. In order to have enough skin, cut the neck of the animal near the shoulders (**Figure 85**).

To obtain an even cut, the Indians passed a cord around the animal's neck and then cut by following this cord. The longest part of the skin of the neck should be that near the legs. Do not cut the neck too short. Never cut the throat, because the incision would be too difficult to conceal with a seam.

FLAYING

1. Start the incision on the top of the neck (**Figure 86**).

2. Work from the base toward the top of the head (**Figure 87**).

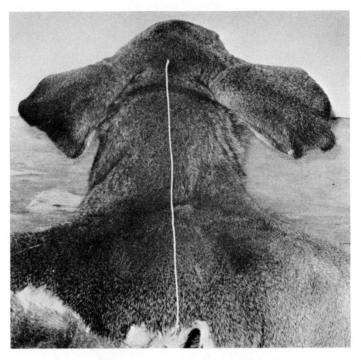

Fig. 87. Area of the incision.

In the case of a head with horns you must make the incision in the form of a Y; each point of the top of the Y should be at the base of a horn (**Figure 88**).

3. Using a screwdriver, detach the skin as far as the base of the ears.

4. Cut the ears very close to the skull (**Figure 89**).

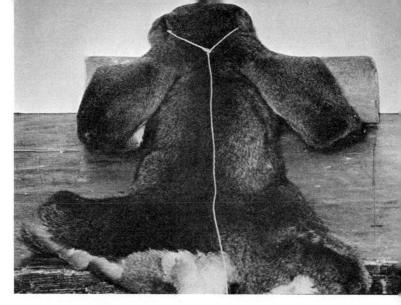

Fig. 88. Incision for a head with horns.

Fig. 89. Cutting the ears.

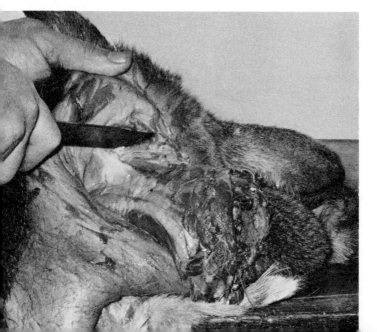

5. Cut off the neck at the base of the skull and continue the flaying, turning back the skin over the head. If there are antlers, cut near the horns because no hairs should remain attached to the base of the antlers.

6. Flay delicately around the eyes, without cutting the eyelashes. For that, insert a finger into the orbital cavity (**Figure 90**) and hold the eyelids with the other fingers of the same hand (**Figure 91**). Then cut around the first finger.

7. Continue the flaying as far as the nostrils and the mouth. Use your finger again to prevent making any cuts in the skin of the mouth. Cut the lips very close to the teeth.

Fig. 90. Placing the finger through the eye opening to avoid cutting the eyelashes.

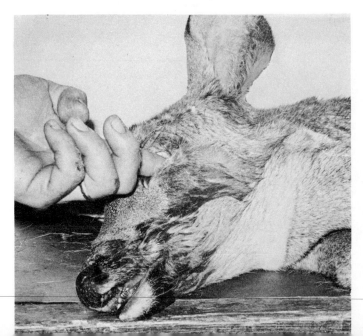

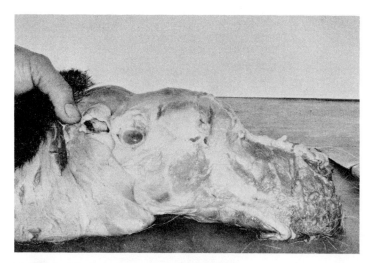

Fig. 91. Skin removed around the eye.

Fig. 92. Skinning the ears.

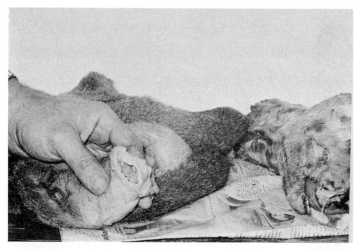

8. Returning to the ears, the skin should be turned back immediately in order to avoid subsequent falling of the hairs (**Figure 92**).

9.   Cut the cartilage and the surplus from the base of the ear (**Figure 93**). Proceed delicately, because the skin is very fragile in this region.

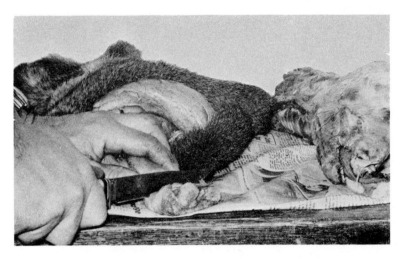

Fig. 93. Cutting the ear cartilage.

Fig. 94. Flaying the ear.

10. Continue to flay the external part of the ear by turning the skin back and forcing it gently with your thumb (**Figure 94**).

11. Be sure that no trace of flesh remains on the ears (**Figures 95 and 96**).

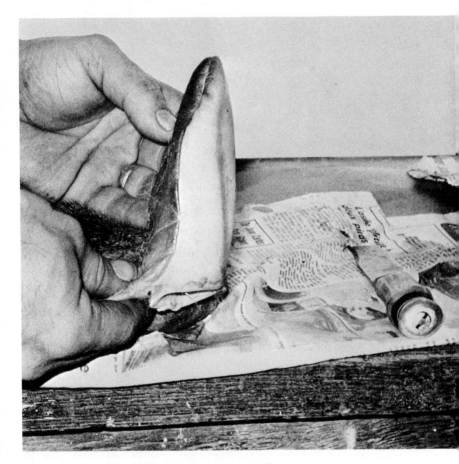

Fig. 95. The flayed ears (a).

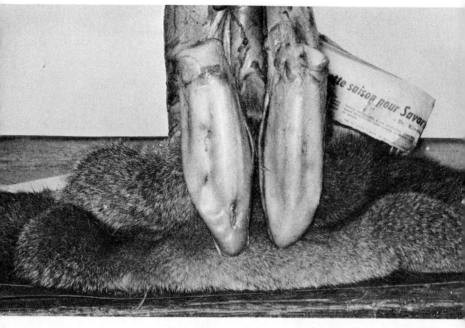

Fig. 96. The flayed ears (b). View from side.

12. Reverse the skin around the neck and remove the flesh with the aid of a knife. Also cut the inside of the lips to within one inch of the corner of the mouth. Delicately remove the flesh from them. Likewise, scrape around the eyelids, taking great care not to cut the eyelashes.

PREPARING THE SKIN

Fasten a piece of wood in a vise. Spread out the reversed skin and scrape the inside carefully. As in Chapter 5, use a plane, or a paintscraper, with rounded corners that will not harm the skin.

Having removed the fat and the flesh, proceed to the salting. Spread out the skin, hairy side down, and distribute the salt over all the bare places; then rub it in well. Roll it up, hairs on the outside, as shown in **Figure 83.**

After about three days — that is to say, the time necessary for the salt to absorb all the blood — wash and rinse the skin, and place it in the tanning solution, where it should remain for at least ten days. For an elk or a caribou, this time should be twenty to twenty-four days.

MOUNTING

Preparation of the Skull

To avoid the work of preparing a natural skull, many taxidermists use papier-mâché forms like the one shown in **Figure 97.** For a head with antlers, the upper part of the natural skull (**Figures 98, 99**) is cut and firmly attached to the bought form. Because these forms are expensive, however, you may wish to prepare the natural skull by using the following procedures:

With a knife, remove the flesh, the eyes, and the tongue. Use a long spoon for the brain. If you have any difficulty, plunge the skull into a caldron of hot water, and let it boil like a soup bone. Stop the boiling when the flesh turns gray. If you boil it too long the skull will separate into several parts. *In the case of a head with antlers, take care that these remain outside of the water.*

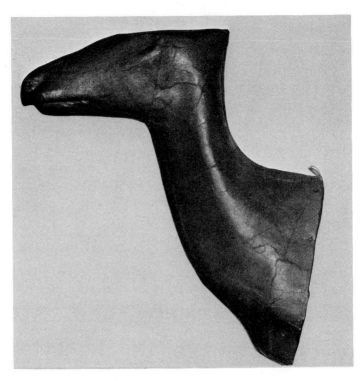

Fig. 97. A commercial form.

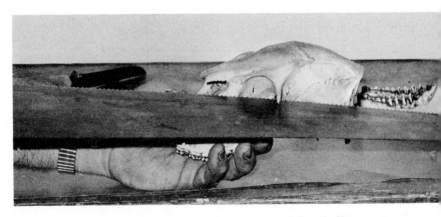

Fig. 98. The upper part of the skull.

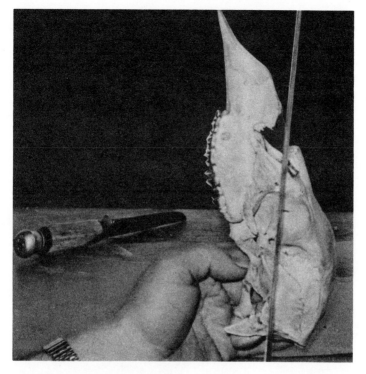

Fig. 99. The upper part of the skull, showing
where to saw a skull with horns.

Mounting with Natural Skull

Use the following materials:

a. A plank of laminated wood, ¾" thick: use a
plank large enough to allow you to cut from it the
plaque for the form of the neck and the base.

b. Straw, tacks, nylon cord, wood screws (1½"

115

long, flat head), papier-mâché.

c. A decorative support to which you will attach the head. To make this perfectly symmetrical, draw half of the pattern in the desired size on a piece of strong cardboard. Then you have only to trace this in reverse for the other half.

Preparing the Skin

1. Take the skin from the tanning solution and treat it as described in Chapter 5. I remind you that you can also simply use a tannery for this difficult work.

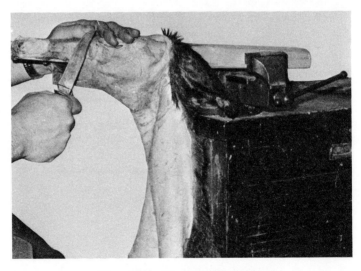

Fig. 100. Fleshing the skin.

2. Reverse the dry skin on a piece of wood, 2" x 3", thinned at one end and held in a vise (Figure 100).

3. Check carefully that no morsels of flesh remain in the nose, around the eyes (look at the eyelashes), and in the lips. The covering of the latter, which will be reconstructed in the mounting, is very fragile. Finally, the skin should be white and free of all fatty matter (**Figure 101**).

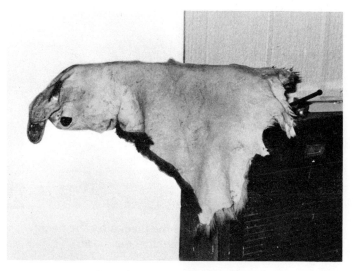

Fig. 101. The prepared skin.

Making the Form

1. Lay the neck, which you have kept, on a sheet of strong paper and draw the outline of it with a pencil. Then saw out a plaque of laminated wood corresponding to this outline.

2. Measure the circumference of the neck at the

base and at the top, and saw a plaque of the same circumference as that of the base. We shall call them:
(a) the plaque for the form of the neck, and (b) the
plaque for the base (**Figure 102**).

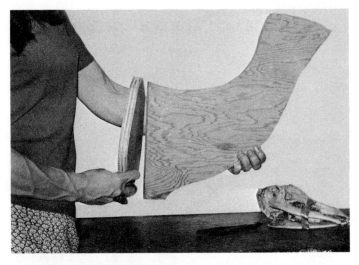

Fig. 102. The form: (a) the plaque for the neck;
(b) the plaque for the base.

3. Before assembling these two plaques, adjust
the skull on the plaque for the form of the neck. To do
this, enlarge the cavity at the base of the skull with
the nippers.

4. Make three holes in the top of the skull, which
will permit you to screw it to the plaque for the form
of the neck (**Figure 103**).

5. Check that the position of the head is correct

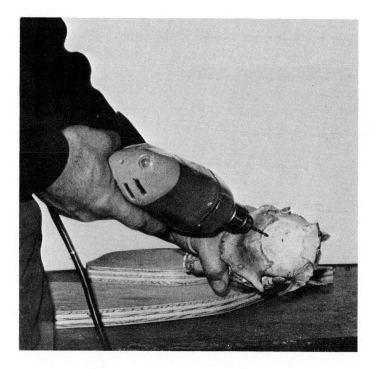

Fig. 103. Making three holes in the top of the skull.

before attaching it definitively.

6. Screw the two plaques together. Be sure they are well centered.

7. Temporarily attach a piece of wood to the back of the base plaque. This will permit you to hold the form in the vise.

8. Cut a support, preferably of pine, that will fill

the nasal cavity and hold up the skin of the nose (**Figures 104 and 105**).

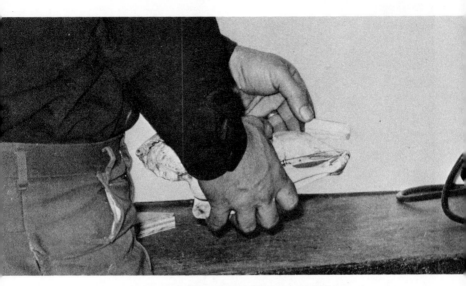

Fig. 104. The nasal filling.

Fig. 105.
The nasal filling
completed.

9. Without embedding them completely, nail some tacks at the top and at the bottom of the plaque for the form of the neck (as in **Figure 106**).

Fig. 106. Rebuilding the skull.

10. Be sure that the skull is firmly screwed to the form.

11. Rebuild the skull with some papier-mâché or modeling clay; the latter is worked more easily if you moisten your fingers often (**Figure 106**).

12. Fill the orbits with modeling clay and place the eyes in position (**Figure 107**).

13. With a knife, cut two holes to represent the

nostrils, on either side of the piece of wood that takes the place of the nose.

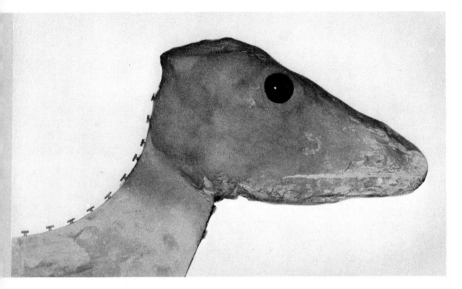

Fig. 107. Placing the eyes.

14. Indent a fairly deep horizontal line on each side of the mouth (**as in Figure 107**).

15. Using straw, cover the plaque for the form of the neck, starting near the skull. Keep the straw in place by lacing a thread from an upper tack to a lower tack. Do just one side at a time. Your form is ready (**Figures 108, 109, 110**).

Placing the Skin

1. Try the skin on the form. Check that the two

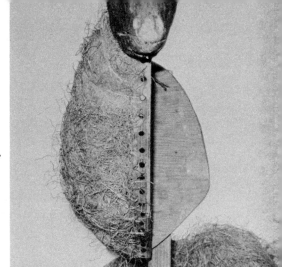

Fig. 108. Placing the straw.

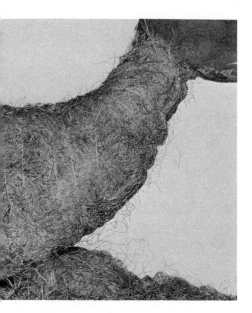

Fig. 109. The curved neck of the form.

Fig. 110. The neck completed.

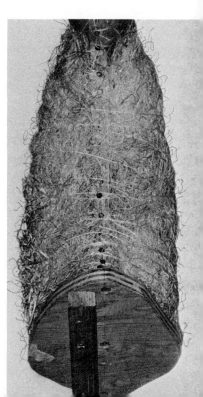

ends can be joined without effort, and that the eyes are well centered. There is still time to make corrections.

2. Fill the covering of the lips with papier-mâché and sew it up.

3. In the covering of each ear, place a piece of cardboard cut according to its shape. (You can buy pre-formed ears, coated with paraffin, which makes them impermeable.)

4. Adjust the skin on the form and hold it in place by means of three cords, knotted on the top

5. Check the correct position of the lips; the upper lip should extend a little.

6. Arrange the nose by lightly inserting a nail within each nostril. Attach the nails to the wooden support of the nose, which you placed previously. Drive the nails with a flat punch, which you hit with a hammer.

7. Be sure that the eyelids are well placed; nail them down temporarily with the points about ¾" apart.

8. Sew up the skin around the form, using a triangular needle and the nylon thread used for fishing (20 lbs. resistance), or shoemaker's thread (waxed end). Start at the base of the neck and make stitches ¼" apart. Do not forget to replace the hairs after each stitch so that the seam will be invisible.

9. Check that the white spot on the throat is well centered.

10. Fold back the excess of skin around the base plaque. Attach it with $\%_{16}''$ hooks and nail it firmly. The skin must never be wrinkled on the form.

11. Check the correct position of the ears and nail them securely to the inside of their base. Sew all around the periphery so that the cardboard, inserted previously, will allow them to dry without being displaced. The thread can be removed after the drying.

12. Some nails buried deep on the top of the skull will be an additional guaranty of firmness, and will be perfectly hidden under the hair.

13. Dilute some hot beeswax with a few drops of turpentine and fill the openings around the eyes. Put a thin layer of this in the nostrils and the ears, and between the lips.

14. Brush the hairs of the head and suspend it in a warm, dry place. The minimum period of drying is fourteen days. Daily checking is required.

Completion

Brush the hairs of the dry head. Mix a few drops of boiled linseed oil with a little paint from a tube, the color of lampblack. Apply this mixture with a very good brush, lightly over the nose and more copiously inside the nostrils.

Cut away the surplus skin that was tucked behind the base plaque. Attach the decorative support by screwing it securely to the base plaque. Hide the heads of the screws with plastic wood. Place a good hook on the back and hang the head wherever it looks good to you.

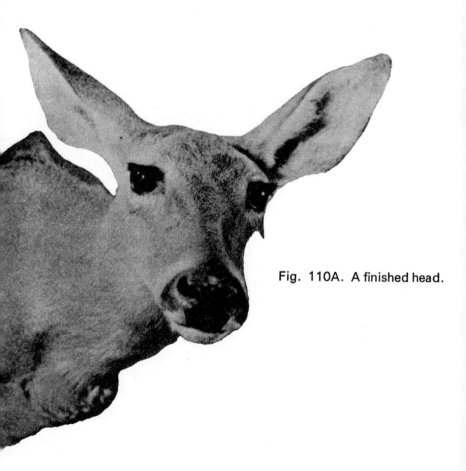

Fig. 110A. A finished head.

Horns and Antlers

HORNS

Such animals as oxen, sheep, goats, and cows have permanent horns — that is, horns that do not fall annually. These horns can be made into ash trays, pen holders, ink stands, and book ends, or serve simply as a decoration for the wall.

Start by separating the horny sheath, or horn, from the bony protuberance of the forehead (the horn socket). To do this, boil the skull for four hours — or let it soak in cold water for three weeks. If you use only part of the skull, saw out the region that you have chosen.

Then, to remove any marks that you consider unattractive, rub the horns first with a rasp, then with sandpaper No. 4, and finally with extra-fine sandpaper No. 00. A layer of liquid wax, of boiled linseed oil, or of glossy varnish will bring out the desired brilliance.

If you wish to attach the horns to a skull, or a part of the skull that you have reserved for this purpose, dilute some Plaster of Paris with a little water to a fairly thick consistency and fill the horns with this before replacing them on their sockets (which have, themselves, been previously cleaned).

ANTLERS

Saw out the upper part of the skull, which carries the antlers, taking into account the effect you wish to produce. Wash the skull section with soap and tepid water.

Fig. 111. A mounted head with antlers.

If you wish to use the skin, take it off before you saw out the piece, and treat it in the usual manner (see Chapter 5).

At the center of the skull, puncture a hole of the diameter of the screw, remembering that the bigger the antlers, the larger must be the size of the screw. The length of the screw must be equal to the thickness of the skull plus that of the support.

Prepare a piece of wood (preferably pine) of the size of the cranial cavity. Cut into this a hole, corresponding to the one made in the skull. Drive in the screw from the top of the skull and across the piece of wood. The threaded part of it that extends beyond will serve to fasten the screw to the decorative support. Shape the skull with Plaster of Paris or papier-mâché. This will allow you to hide the head of the screw. Allow the shaping to dry.

Prepare the support. Do not forget to attach a loop to it so that you can hang it later.

If you make use of the skin, take it out of the tanning solution and try it on the skull. Otherwise you can mask the bareness of the skull with a piece of very thin leather, or with a coat of paint.

Screw the skull and its antlers to the decorative support. The screw nut, tightened forcefully, should be fitted into the back of the support, and hidden with plastic wood. Liquid wax or boiled linseed oil will restore the luster to the antlers. (See Figures 112 and 112A.)

Fig. 112. Mounted antlers of a deer.

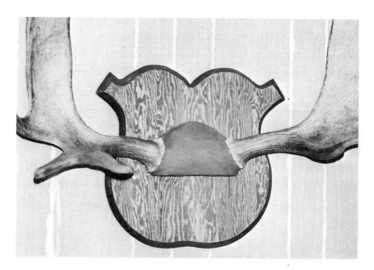

Fig. 112A. Mounted antlers of a bull moose.

Rugs

FOR rugs you should use pelts of good quality and beautiful appearance. In this chapter we will treat the skin of a black bear, a pelt that gives excellent results. You would proceed in the same manner with a white bear.

PREPARATION

Start by flaying the animal very closely, because the skin of a bear is very fat. Make an incision under each leg so that the flesh can be well removed.

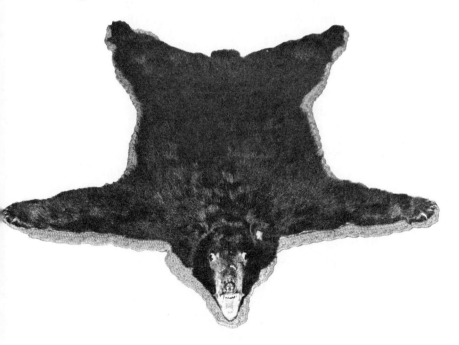

Fig. 113. A bear rug.

For the head, proceed in the same manner as for a deer, but without cutting the skin of the neck. Pay particular attention to the ears and to the periphery of the eyes.

If you cannot obtain the services of a tannery, proceed to the scraping, salting, and immersion in tanning solution, as described in Chapter 5. Then stretch the skin for at least eight consecutive hours — that is, until it is completely dry.

Remove the grease from the fur by spreading the skin on the ground, or on a panel of wood, slightly inclined. Wash the skin with cold water and a cake of soap; do this at least four times. Then rinse it one last time with cold water from a hose. Let the skin drain.

The Skull

While this is going on, prepare the skull. Place a piece of pine below the mouth and tie the wood and the mouth together firmly. Insert another piece of wood between the jaws, which will allow the animal to have its mouth wide open. Reconstruct the skull with papier-mâché — or with modeling clay, which is heavier. In working with the latter, moisten your fingers continually.

Nail an artificial tongue inside the mouth. This tongue is a reproduction, in wood or papier-mâché, of the original tongue.

Put some papier-mâché between the lips and the gums, as well as at the back of the mouth. Place the eyes in position.

Completion

During these preparations the skin will have dried somewhat. Nail or hook it, hairy side up, all around the periphery, stretching it well. To do this, start at the midline of the back and go completely around, one-half inch from the edge. Place the feet in good positions. Brush the fur against the direction of growth of the hair.

Now straighten the skull, the position of the feet, the eyes, the ears, and so forth. Rebuild the inside of the feet and fix the claws, slightly spread, with adhesive tape and small nails.

For the drying, allow twenty days for the skin of a black bear weighing about 150 pounds. At the end of this time, take out the hooks or nails and sand the skin, remembering that the more you sand it the more supple it will be.

Line the skin with a burgundy red or very light red cloth, allowing this to extend about two inches all around. This lining can be either glued or sewn. The ideal material is felt; but you can also use a crocheted or knitted edging. Brush the hair one last time.

Put a little beeswax in the nostrils, around the gums, and around the eyes. The teeth can be cleaned in the usual way. Paint the tongue, and the inside of the mouth, trying to make them appear as nearly alive as possible. Find help in color photographs that you have taken.

The result should resemble **Figure 113.**

Mounting the Legs of Mammals

THE legs of deer, caribou, and elk will make feet for tables, handles for knives, coat racks, gun racks, and mountings for ash trays. Grouped in three or four, they will form the base of a bedside lamp (**Figure 114**).

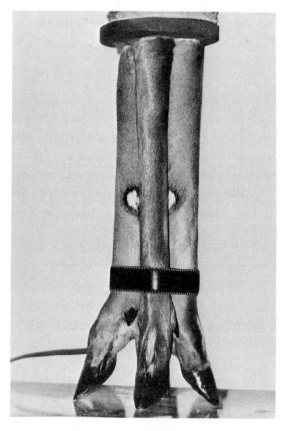

Fig. 114. Mounted legs.

Use the forelegs, which are often more attractive. Cut the legs off at the knee; you can keep them in the freezer until you are ready to work on them.

SKINNING

1. Lean the leg on the table and, with a good hunting knife or a sharp penknife, make an incision in the back of it (**Figure 115**).

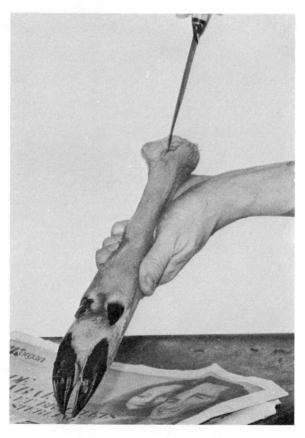

Fig. 115. Making the incision.

2. Loosen the skin and leave as little flesh as possible (**Figure 116–117**).

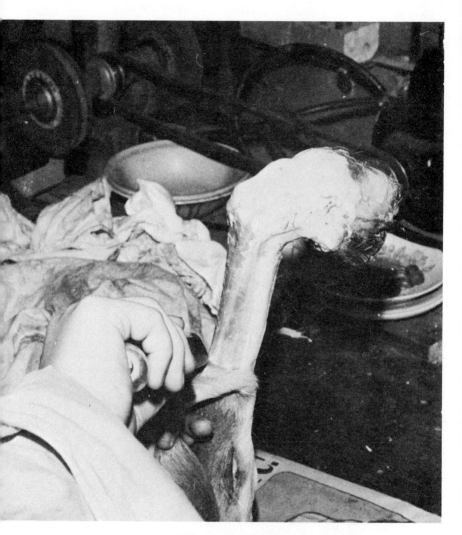

Fig. 116. Skinning the leg (a).

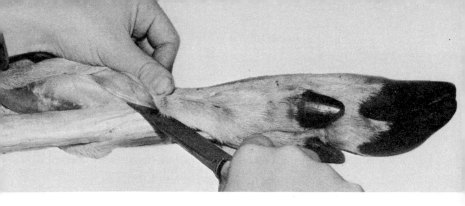

Fig. 117. Skinning the leg (b).

3. When you reach the height of the spurs, cut the ligaments at the joint of the latter; they thus remain attached to the skin (**Figure 118**).

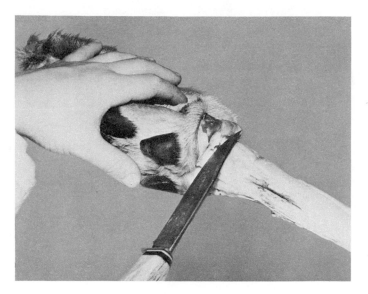

Fig. 118. Cutting at the spurs.

4. Continue skinning as far as the joint of the hoof.

5. Cut the ligaments that hold the bone of the leg.

6. Remove the bone and set it aside (**Figure 119**). It will serve you as model for the form.

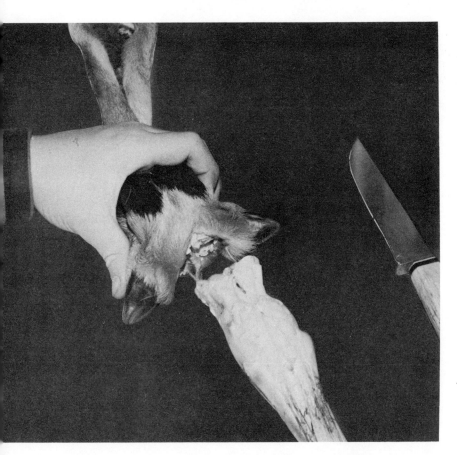

Fig. 119. Removing the leg bone.

PREPARING THE SKIN

Free the skin of its last shreds of flesh and rub it generously with table salt (**Figure 120**). Be particular about the joint of the hoof (**Figure 121**). Roll up the skin, hairs inside, and wrap it in a wet cloth.

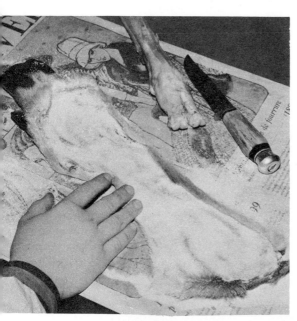

Fig. 120.
Salting the skin.

Fig. 121.
Salting at the
base of the hoofs.

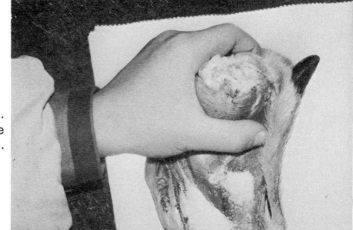

Wait at least two days. Then unroll the skin and remove the flesh that the salt will have dried. Wash and rinse in cold water, and plunge the skin into the tanning solution. Allow it to remain for at least seven days, stirring it daily for a few minutes. Then take the skin from the solution and rinse it in cold water.

THE FORM

In the meantime prepare the form. Use pine which, although it is a little more expensive than spruce, offers less risk of cracking.

The size of the form depends on the original leg. It should be slightly smaller than the bone that was removed, because the skin always shrinks a little. The skin, moreover, should extend an inch or two beyond the form. Once the skin is dry, this excess will be cut off.

Use a plane to perfect the form. When it is in place sew up the incision with shoemaker's thread starting at the base of the leg.

Let the leg dry for ten days. As a finish, you can apply one or two coats of ironing wax to the hoofs.

Fish

ONE day, perhaps, you will have the desire to stuff a fish as in **Figure 122.** Certain fish, such as the trout, require extremely delicate work, because the scales become slippery and gluey from a mucus secreted by the skin. The latter is so thin that one must be an expert taxidermist to succeed in stuffing it. A mold of Plaster of Paris is necessary for this.

To illustrate these few instructions, I have chosen a 1-lb. perch; it could just as well be a pike. When fishing, do not fail to photograph your specimen as soon as it leaves the water. That will serve you when you come to restore the colors.

SKINNING

Examine the specimen carefully and select for the visible side the one that shows the most scales; or, as a general rule, the one that is less damaged. Place the fish on heavy brown paper and carefully draw the outline of it with a pencil. This will serve you when you are making the form.

Fig. 122.
A mounted perch.

Then lay the fish on a large piece of cheesecloth (never on paper), with the display side down.

1. Cut along the side, from under the pectoral fin as far as the caudal fin (**Figure 123**). End with a vertical incision.

Fig. 123. The incision.

2. Cut the bone at the base of the tail (**Figure 124**).

3. Separate the skin from the body: Use a nipper or a good pair of scissors. Working from the inside, cut the dorsal, anal, ventral, and pectoral fins, as well as the flesh attached to the caudal fin (**Figures 125–127**).

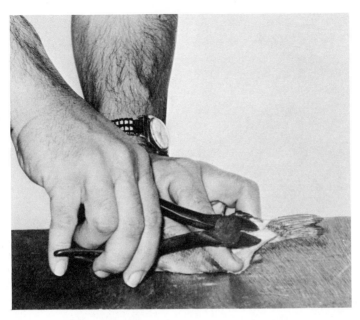

Fig. 124. Cutting the bone at the base of the tail.

Fig. 125. Cutting the fins (a).

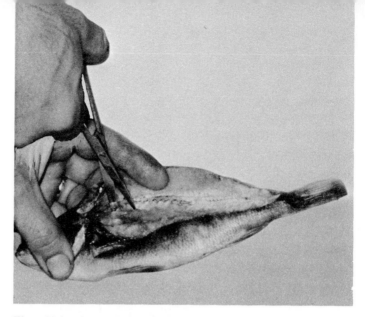

Fig. 126. Cutting the fins (b).

Fig. 127. Cutting the fins (c).

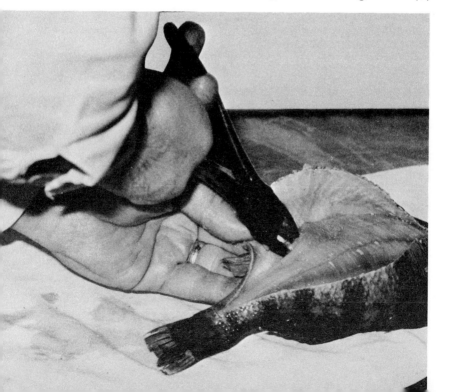

Fig. 128. Cutting the bone behind the gill.

4. Continue the incision toward the head and cut the big bone behind the gill (**Figure 128**).

5. The head remains attached to one side of the skin (**Figure 129**).

Fig. 129. Removing the skin.

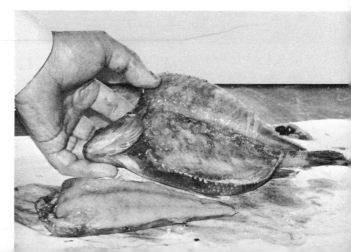

6. Scrape off the excess of flesh with a small spoon (**Figure 130**).

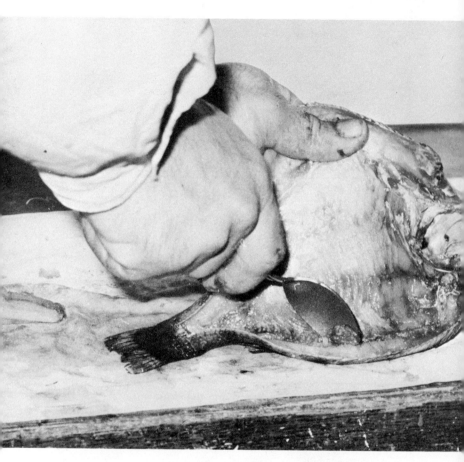

Fig. 130. Removing excess flesh.

7. Take out the tongue and the eyes, and empty the skull (**Figure 131**).

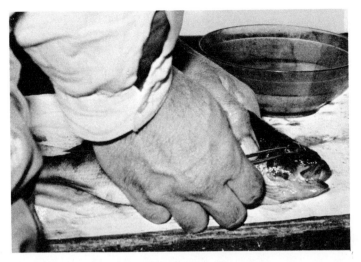

Fig. 131. Removing the eyes.

8. Wash the skin in cold water, using a customary household detergent.

9. Rinse the skin in cold water and wrap it in a damp cloth before putting it in the refrigerator (**Figure 132**).

Fig. 132. Wrapping the skin.

MAKING THE FORM

Using the outline on the brown paper, trace the form on a plank of laminated wood, ¾" thick (as was used for the deer's head); or on a piece of styrofoam (**Figure 133**). The form should be slightly smaller than the model, and without the head and the tail, so that it can be placed within the skin.

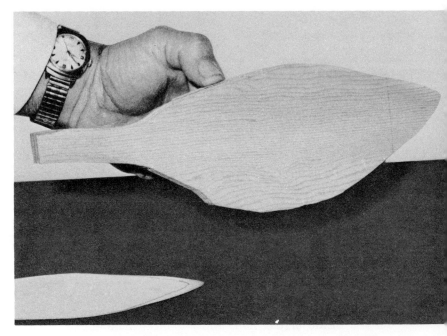

Fig. 133. The form.

Round off the edges of the form, first with a rasp, and then finish with sandpaper No. 00. Screw a small piece of wood to the back of this solid form. This will permit you to nail the skin on one side and attach it to the decorative support on the other side.

MOUNTING

Take the skin from the refrigerator and run it through cold water. When it has thawed wipe the inside with a dry cloth in order to remove all excess water, and sprinkle the inside with borax (**Figure 134**). Fit the skin on the form.

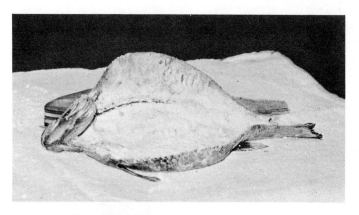

Fig. 134. Applying the borax powder.

On the inside of the skin, apply a little modeling clay at the places for the fins, and fill the holes with a little straw or papier-mâché.

Replace the form inside the skin and check that you can bring the two sides of the incision together. Nail the two sides to the form, starting at the center (**Figure 135**).

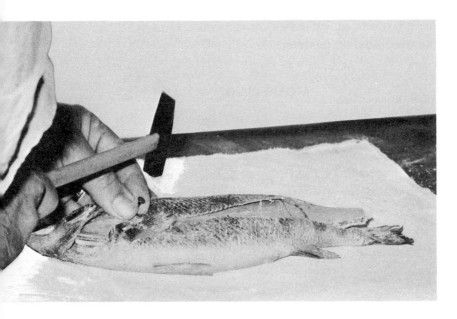

Fig. 135. Nailing the skin to the form.

Fig. 136. Pinning the fins.

Pack the bottom of the mouth with Plaster of Paris, papier-mâché, or modeling clay. If the mouth is to be closed, tie it up now. But if you wish to have it open, keep it in this position by placing a small piece of wood between the jaws.

Preparation for Drying

Place some pieces of flexible plastic or cardboard, held by pins stuck into the base of each fin (**Figure 136**). These will keep the fins open during the drying (**Figure 137**).

The drying should last at least 25 days in a dry place. Rest the fish on a ventilated netting, or a lattice of fiber glass, which will facilitate the circulation of air. Check the condition of the specimen daily, because it

Fig. 137. Mounting for drying.

is always possible to make minor corrections before it is completely solidified.

Restoring of Colors

When the fish is dry, make some holes in the decorative support and screw the fish to it. Put a little modeling clay in the orbit, which you will see once the stuffing is finished. If, however, the fish is to have the head slightly turned so that both eyes are visible, put some clay into the other orbit as well. Then place the eye or eyes in position.

Paint the specimen to look as much as possible like a living fish. Refer to the colored photographs that you have taken. Paint only the visible side. Make these finishing touches slowly. Have several very fine brushes, which will allow you to utilize several colors simultaneously without having either to mix them, or to clean your brush after each change.

If the fish has its mouth open, paint it inside, and when the paint is dry, varnish it. At least four very light coatings of glossy varnish of good quality will be necessary. Apply these at six-hour intervals.

Find the ideal spot to hang your fish and receive the congratulations you deserve.

Now It's Your Turn

AT this point you should proceed on your own to the stuffing of our last specimen — a muskrat. Give particular attention to the tail, which is particularly difficult to work on. **Figures 138–145** will guide you.

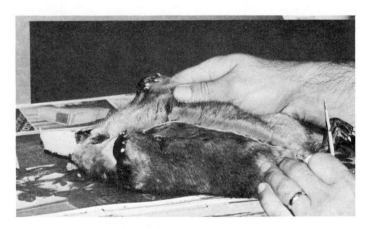

Fig. 138. Spreading the skin.

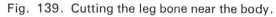
Fig. 139. Cutting the leg bone near the body.

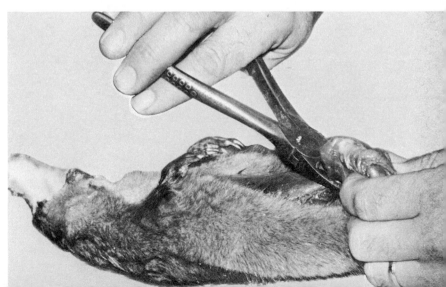

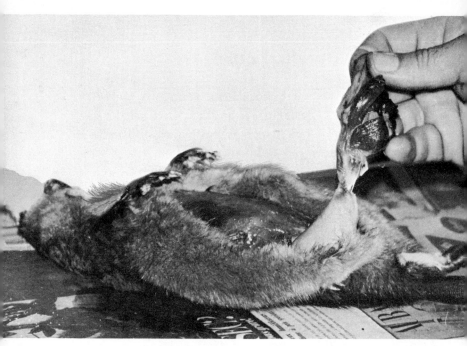

Fig. 140. Leg bone and flesh detached from the body.

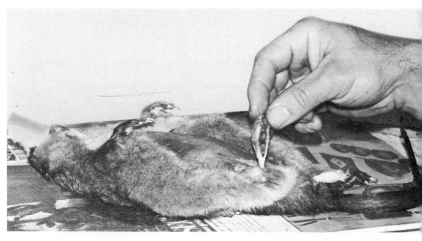

Fig. 141. Flesh removed from leg bone.

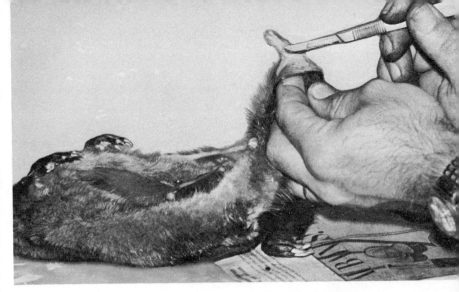

Fig. 142. Skinning the foot.

Fig. 143. The tail incision.

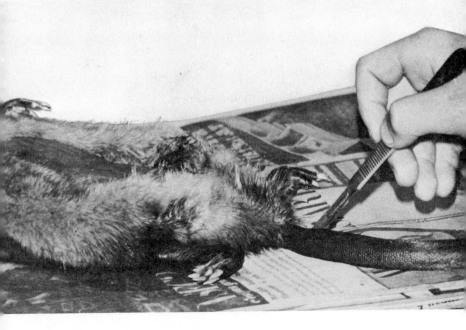

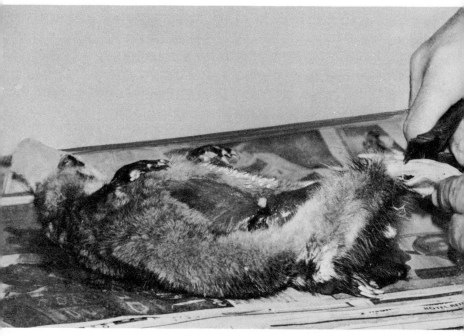

Fig. 144. Cutting the nerve of the tail.

Fig. 145. The finished specimen.